Sharon Osbourne was born in London in 1952. She is married to rock legend Ozzy Osbourne and has three children: Aimee, Kelly and Jack. She divides her time between Los Angeles and Buckinghamshire.

'More no-holds barred revelations'

*Heat* ★★★★★

'The formidable Mrs O is just as honest and open in this second instalment of her life story as the first . . . a real page-turner'

*Woman*

'Shazza goes even deeper to reveal the secrets behind the headlines'

*Look*

'Like *Extreme*, *Survivor* is eye-wateringly frank and very funny.

*Evening Standard*

*Also by Sharon Osbourne*

Extreme

# Sharon Osbourne

# SURVIVOR

SPHERE

First published in Great Britain in 2007 by Sphere
This paperback edition published in 2008 by Sphere

A CIP catalogue record for this book
is available from the British Library.

ISBN 978-0-7515-4054-3

Typeset in Bembo by M Rules
Printed and bound in Great Britain by
Clays Ltd, St Ives plc

Sphere
An imprint of
Little, Brown Book Group
100 Victoria Embankment
London EC4Y 0DY

An Hachette Livre UK Company
www.hachettelivre.co.uk

www.littlebrown.co.uk

This book is dedicated to Minnie:
she's my best friend, my companion,
my confidante and the best gift
I have ever had in my whole life

# Contents

# Sharon Osbourne

---

## SURVIVOR

# Introduction

Sometimes, when you're reading a magazine at the end of a hard day, somebody comes into the room and turns on a light and only then do you realise how dark it has become and you wonder how you've been able to see anything at all. Well, that was how it felt after writing my autobiography, *Extreme*. Being made to look at my past, at things I had buried for so long, brought home to me the level of darkness that had become the norm in my life – but I needed the light to be turned on to see it. That light was Ozzy's sobriety. With it my life changed. As I finished writing the last few pages of the book, my husband was celebrating one whole year of being sober and clean, the first time I had known him that way since we met in 1970 when I was seventeen and he was a loony with a tap around his neck and no socks, squatting on the floor in my father's office where I was working as a receptionist.

The Ozzy I fell in love with, married and chose to be the father of my children was an addict long before we even met. He did everything and anything the pharmaceutical industry could throw at him except heroin. In a recent programme on Channel 4, he topped the poll of drug-crazed musicians who by all the laws of nature shouldn't be alive.

Strange as this may seem, I didn't see this as a problem at the time. It went with the territory, a territory I was literally born into: that old cliché of sex, drugs and rock and roll. The chaos, the craziness – it all seemed normal to me. It's only when you come out the other side that you think, Oh my God. How did we survive that?

It's been over two years since we celebrated Ozzy's first incredible year of no booze and no drugs on 21 April 2005. That milestone – so unbelievable at the time – is now long gone. In that first year there had been wobbly moments, mornings when I would wake up with my instinct saying something wasn't right and the tension running through me like the high-pitched hum of an electricity pylon. I would get through the day in a state of panic, snapping at anyone who came near me, even Minnie, my Pomeranian – the only one, naturally, who would snap back. I would worry myself sick when we were apart, just as I had worried myself sick about the children when they were small, convinced that if I wasn't with them something bad was sure to happen.

For the first couple of years my husband went to an AA meeting every day. It seemed to me that those meetings with other recovering alcoholics were like a substitute drug for him. He needed them. As for me, I was terrified that if he missed even one he might say fuck it and give it all up, as had happened so many times in the past, and I'd find myself once again in that dark place I had only just emerged from. He didn't. Gradually the not-drinking, the not-chucking-painkillers-down-his-throat-as-if-they-were-tic-tacs, became more natural both to him and to those around him. These days, although he still does his meetings, he doesn't need them in the same way and they're no longer every day. Best of all, my husband has a hit record. Not only does that give him a high better than any drug invented, it's proof to him (and to the rest of the world) of what I have been saying all along: that he doesn't need outside stimulants to release his creativity.

In the autumn of 2005 I had my own project to worry about. Let nobody tell you writing an autobiography is easy. I was always determined to be honest, but this decision came at a cost. People's memories of the same event can be surprisingly different, even things that appear relatively straightforward, like the story of a fight my husband and I had in New York in the mid-eighties at the Hard Rock Café – inevitably it was while Ozzy was working on an album, when he was at his most belligerent and difficult. Four people there that night came up with four different versions of what happened, and that's not counting Ozzy himself, who has no memory of the evening at all.

Of all the people whose reaction has been, 'No, you're wrong, it wasn't like that', the most upsetting for me has been my brother. Even though we shared our childhood and adolescence, from poverty in Brixton to diamonds and racehorses in Mayfair and Wimbledon, his memory of those early years is very different from mine. Ask him if he was happy and he'll say yes. From the moment he was born, David adored my mother and she adored him and David is still angry with me at my depiction of her.

He sent me a letter at the time of publication telling me how hurt he was. But, as I wrote at the beginning of the book, 'Memory is a strange thing . . . What follows is only my memory of what happened in my life. I cannot say this is how it happened. I can only say this is how it seemed to me at the time.'

He wrote that he didn't understand why I had only put in the bad things. He had a point. I didn't write about how he had been good to me when I had cancer. And he was. He was really supportive, and I didn't write about that. He said I sounded very bitter in the book. Well, that's his opinion and he's entitled to it. But the bad things were true and that's what I felt.

As it is, our lives have taken very different trajectories. I know that my brother is with his family and I wish him health, wealth and happiness his entire life. The bottom line is that we are so terribly different, and each time in our lives when we try to be friendly and get on, it ends in tears, and I just don't want to cry any more.

It's so hard when you want to be truthful not to hurt other people, and my husband – the person I least want to hurt in the world – hasn't even dared read *Extreme* because he's so frightened he comes out badly. But as anyone who has read my first book will know, he doesn't. On the contrary: he comes out as the crazy, loving, gorgeous man he is, with that extraordinary sense of humour that most women will agree is the ultimate aphrodisiac.

I, too, was frightened as the day of publication approached, but for a different reason. I didn't want to look a fool. I was never convinced that my story would interest anybody. It was only my life, after all, a life I suspected should be subtitled 'a cautionary tale'. But readers themselves proved me wrong. In early 2006 it was named the biggest-selling autobiography since records began, and a couple of months later it won Biography of the Year at the British Book Awards.

Did writing it change me? Well, something did. It allowed me to look at my life from the outside and see patterns I hadn't been aware of before. As a child – and even later – I often felt like I was acting out a story, and I would sometimes dramatise what was happening to make it more interesting. But I had no sense of whether it was a comedy or a tragedy. Now I realise it was a mixture of the two.

It didn't happen all at once, but light began to creep into my life, like sunshine forces its way through the blinds in mid-summer. I began to sleep better, and one morning I woke up and decided I couldn't stand living in gloom and clutter any more. So I set to work on the house in Beverly Hills, made famous in *The Osbournes*. Doors that for years had looked like they led to dungeons were painted as white as vanilla ice cream. Windows, tinted by MTV for the show, were stripped of their smoked-glass coating, and for the first time since we moved in, the kitchen was flooded with natural light. You could pick up a magazine and read it without turning on a lamp.

The kids loved the new look. Everyone loved it. Everyone except Ozzy, who said it looked like a hospital. As for the hall, which was done a distressed pale blue, he said, 'It looks as if someone's wiped their arse on it.' As my friend Gloria always says, 'Men never like change.'

But the light couldn't reach every corner. When I finished writing *Extreme*, it felt as if I had closed the book on a set of accounts that for years I hadn't been able to balance, and to some extent I still feel that's the case. But I hadn't resolved everything – I don't think anybody can, just like that – and there was still so much I'd stuffed away. Issues with my health, my body, my role as a mother now that the kids were growing up and leaving home. And my relationship with my father, who had always been such a huge figure in my life, and was now seriously ill with Alzheimer's.

## Introduction

The fact is, life never quite goes according to plan. You'd think as an Osbourne I would have realised that by now. Yet, although I didn't know it at the time, I was about to enter one of the most turbulent periods of my life.

# Hollywood

Summer 2007. Another sun-drenched day in LA. Outside, the traffic moves slowly up Hollywood Boulevard, the side-walks empty except for tourists and office workers on their way from lunch, keeping to the shade, talking into their cell phones, getting on with their lives. But inside my father's nursing home it's another world. An oasis of calm. My heels click on the polished floor as I walk down the corridor towards his room, past closed doors. A nurse smiles at me. I don't recognise her. It's been a while since I was last here. My schedule these last few months has been insane, just madness, even for me. Launching my husband's new album and a massive world tour. Filming *The X-Factor* and *America's Got Talent*. Getting Ozzfest up and running for another year. There's never enough time.

A wave of guilt washes over me, like it always does when I come here. I should visit more often. What kind of a daughter am I?

My father Don Arden – the legendary rock manager – had already been diagnosed with Alzheimer's when he came back into my life six years ago. At that point he could understand maybe 50 per cent of what you said, but in the last three years he's really deteriorated. It's such a cruel and pitiless illness. Terrifying. Most old people retreat into their memories, but he had been robbed even of that. As Don's condition got worse we had to move him here, into Belmont, and now he needs care twenty-four hours a day. The bills are crippling, but that's OK. My father took care of me when I was a child. Now he's like a child himself, so I take care of him. That's how it should be.

I hear the music before I even walk into the room. Pavarotti. My father was a huge fan, and I had taken him to see the great tenor in concert in Vegas shortly before we had to move him into Belmont. I do believe that even people in the worst stages of Alzheimer's can pick up an atmosphere. Maybe more so than the rest of us. The music is so calming and relaxing. I'm sure it helps. As my father was getting worse, if there was a sudden, loud noise on the TV, or the dogs started barking he would become totally afraid. Fear has a strange effect on people with dementia and, like a lot of fellow sufferers, my father can get violent, sometimes lashing out at the nurses when they were changing his diaper. And not just the staff. One time he wandered into the wrong room by mistake and another patient – an old lady – threw a cup at him, so he went over and slapped her. It wasn't his fault: he was frightened, just like she was. He needs calm. He needs routine. And he's always loved music.

My father is sitting in his wheelchair. Just after Christmas he fell – nobody quite knows how – and he never regained the use of his legs. He's wearing his tracksuit bottoms, the ones we gave him with the Ozzy logo. He would never have dreamed of wearing a tracksuit before he got sick. My father was so particular about everything. He would shower three times a day. He would change his clothes three times a day. Everything was pristine; his appearance was immaculate. He bought nothing off the hanger; everything was tailor made. But the tracksuits are comfortable and make things easier for the nurses.

'Hi Dad. It's Shah.'

No response. Not a flicker of recognition in his eyes. I pull up an easy chair and sit next to him. He's been like this for over a year. Over a year since I've seen an emotion cross his face. He doesn't know who I am; I'm not even sure if he knows I'm here.

Ozzy sees it differently. The last time he came with me to visit, he was sure Don recognised him. 'He knows it's me, Sharon. I can see it in his eyes. I promise you, he looked straight at me.' And I was like, Fuck off, he's not looking at you, he's looking through you, at someone imaginary over there in the corner. Ozzy was utterly convinced, but I know. I'm absolutely certain he doesn't recognise me. And that's not going to change now.

So what am I doing? Why did I come? Sometimes I wonder what the point is. He doesn't know I'm here; it doesn't even register. Hardly anyone visits him any more. All his old friends and cronies – they've abandoned him, or are dead themselves. Only his mistress Meredith has stayed loyal. She still visits him every week. My brother David used to, but he has had to move back to England. One way or another, Don's family are all estranged or back in Manchester like his sister Eileen.

There's really only Dari I can count on. Dari originally came to our house in Beverly Hills to help with the laundry and the ironing when the children were still small. She comes from Georgia in the south of what was the Soviet Union – by one of those strange coincidences, not far from where my father's family came from originally. In her country she was a fully qualified doctor, but the way things work in America, she couldn't carry on in her profession without re-studying and taking new exams. From my point of view, Dari has been a godsend. She's been caring for Don for over two years now. When I'm away, she keeps me up to date. She tells me how 'Mr Don' is doing, checks that he is being given the care I've asked for, and that's as much as anybody could do.

As for me, his daughter, I could visit every day or stay away for good – neither would make any difference to Don, I'm sure of it. So why *am* I here? It's not just a sense of duty. I've been thinking about this for a while now. I've come here today for a particular reason.

# Hollywood

A few months ago I had taken a call from Pamela Stephenson, Billy Connolly's beautiful, funny and clever wife, who gave up performing to train as a psychologist. She now practises professionally in New York. She wanted me to take part in a new TV show she was working on called *Shrink Rap*. It was done like a therapy session, looking at how your childhood had influenced your life. She had her sights on a handful of people who'd written or talked in public about how their past had affected their lives.

I still don't really know why I agreed to do it, but before I knew what had happened it was fixed. There was a date and a time down in the diary and that was that. By then everyone was telling me, 'Are you mad?! You've gotta get out of it!' My brilliant and very loyal PA Melinda was saying: 'It's easy, Sharon. Just say no.' But I'd made a promise to Ms Connolly, as she calls herself professionally, and there was nothing I could do about it. I buried my head in the sand, as I so often do, and hoped she would just go away and find somebody else to play with. Even on the morning itself Jude – who does my hair and make-up whenever I am in LA – was saying, 'Let's just run!' But I was too much of a coward to do that either.

I found the whole experience very weird. Everybody took it extremely seriously. The crew all had to sign a confidentiality contract, and when you were being filmed, only the sound man and two camera guys were on set. Everyone else was kept out of the studio. Of course I knew they were all watching it on the monitors, but then I'm just an old cynic.

13

The whole thing went on for about three and a half hours, which they cut down to forty-three minutes for the programme. And, I have to say, Pamela was very supportive after the show was recorded. It wasn't like, 'Right, that's it, we've got what we need. Bye.' She called up several times afterwards to talk things through and see how I was. And she would have taken anything out I didn't want. But once I'd done it, it was like, Oh fuck it, I'm walking away.

Melinda had come with me and going back in the car she said, 'I really don't think that should go out. I think you should can it. Save it for your memoirs.' She had called Michael Guarracino at my LA office while I was in there with Pamela: 'This is going horribly wrong,' she had said. 'If I could stop the interview I would. She is in bits on camera and it is horrible.'

When the show aired, some of my friends were horrified on my behalf. They couldn't understand why I did it. They thought it was humiliating to show myself on TV like that. Crying. Vulnerable. I've always been very upfront and frank. I can't help it. It's how I am. At the end of the session, Pamela thanked me for 'speaking from the heart'. I just laughed and said, 'I can't speak any other way.' And it's true, I can't. Sometimes I wish I could. Sometimes it gets me into trouble.

People have asked me whether I found the experience cathartic. Fuck no! It was like, For fuck's sake, maybe now I can get some peace. You can't expect any mind-changing revelations in three and a half hours. For mind-changing revelations you need years of therapy and it takes a real commitment. There isn't a Botox equivalent for sorting out your head.

Even so, I found myself thinking about everything we'd discussed. Having delved into my past so recently for the book, a lot of what we talked about was familiar territory, but she still brought me to tears – though that's not hard to do.

We talked about my mother, and how I felt we never really had a connection. About Ozzy and how he saved me. He'd loved me, he'd needed me, and I'd blossomed because of him. I would never have survived without him. Until I met him, I was just a precocious brat. Brash, big-mouthed, violent. (Pamela didn't like it when I said that – she thought I was being too hard on myself. But it was true. Ozzy made me a better person because he loved me unconditionally.) We talked about my three gorgeous children and why they are the most precious things in the world to me.

And we talked about my father.

In preparation for the show, Pamela read my autobiography, and towards the end of the session she told me that knowing what she now did, she was astounded that I had come through at all. I remember feeling surprised. Then, in just a couple of sentences, she listed what my father had done: made me lie for him, cheat for him, steal for him. He had betrayed me, threatened to kill me, threatened to kill my children. 'I don't know how you survived it, Sharon,' Pamela said. 'I really don't.' Yet I did more than survive. I flourished. I suppose it's like when you see speeded-up traffic on film: you wonder why the cars don't crash into each other, yet somehow they don't.

There was one thing that really surprised me. We were talking about my father, the fact that he was in a rest home and that I was the one looking after him.

'Why are you supporting him?' she asked. 'Are you still seeking his approval?' I had never thought of it like that and the idea quite shocked me. As for the question why: I don't know. Sometimes I wonder if maybe I'm doing it so people will say, 'Isn't she great; what a great woman she is, taking him back!' I suppose I bothered because I couldn't have lived with myself if I hadn't. What would have happened to him? Penniless in Los Angeles? Without me footing the bills he'd have been on Skid Row. Destitute. How could I have lived with that?

It got me thinking, though. Something Pamela said really stuck with me – that it's 'normal to protect our abusers'. I'd never heard of that before, but now I can't help wondering if that's what I'm doing.

I don't want to sound bitter, like my brother said. My father may have betrayed me, and some people thought he was a monster, but he wasn't all bad. He taught me a lot. So much! He taught me how to be a fighter. It's because of him that I'm not afraid of anyone.

I just want to try to understand before it's too late. There are so many questions I never got to ask him. He can't answer them now; he can't even understand what I'm saying, doesn't recognise me or anybody. But maybe if I sit here with him I can work a few things out for myself. Because it's only when you start to understand someone that you can begin to forgive them.

# Hollywood

I reach out and take my father's hand. Nothing, no response. His nails are dirty – I make sure he gets a manicure once a week but you know how it is. It's not the nurses' fault. He would have hated it, though. If he could see what he's become, he'd just die. He'd go insane.

I just pray he really doesn't know what's happening to him, that Ozzy's wrong and he's not trying to communicate. I know what it's like to be alive in a body and not be able to tell anyone. One time during one of my operations I woke up from the anaesthetic. I couldn't move my eyes; I could hear everything that was going on but I couldn't move my body. I couldn't signal to anyone what was happening. It was one of the most terrifying experiences of my life. Terrible.

There we are, spending our lives imagining we're in control of our bodies but we're not, not in the end. If my father's condition has taught me anything, then it's this. He used to be such a powerful man, so well built and strong. It was like there was a force field all around him. And now it's as if he's shrunk; he's just this little old man.

I've spent my whole life fighting with my body, fighting the years. You can be the strongest, fittest person, but whatever you manage to do, it's only temporary. I'm just starting to learn that. All these years I've waged a war on my body, and now here's my father sitting in front of me, reminding me it's a war you can never win. Not in the end.

# 1

## Growing Old Disgracefully

In the autumn of 2005 I was busier than I had ever been in my life. Ozzfest might have been over for another year, but the second series of *The X-Factor* was about to air and my autobiography was hitting the bookshops. Jonathan Ross asked me on to his TV show to talk about the book, and in the process I managed to scandalise the more po-faced newspapers by getting him to feel my new tits.

At the end of the nineties I had been seriously overweight and had undergone a surgical procedure to limit my food intake: I had a gastric band put round my stomach. A year later I'd lost 125 pounds – about eight and a half stone. Although most of the fat had gone, the excess skin hadn't, so I needed plastic surgery. I had nearly everything done – cut, sucked and lifted – including my breasts, which had been a ridiculous size and looked like two balloons filled with water. After the operation they were a perfectly respectable 34C.

Seven years on and gravity had taken its toll. My tits were looking their age and I decided they needed a revamp. It wasn't that simple, the surgeon told me. Because they were so broad, if they were just lifted – the nipple moved, the excess cut away – I'd end up with a couple of dinner plates on either side of my chest. I'd need implants to give them shape, he said. For a more natural look he suggested pouches filled with saline rather than silicone, inserted in front of the muscle, easier to do and less painful. So that's what happened. It all passed off very smoothly. A bit of pain – nothing like this is totally pain free – but acceptable, and I just loved them. There they were as perky as a twenty-year-old's, now a nice bouncy 34D and I was ridiculously proud of them. Jonathan seemed to like them too.

As the old saying has it, pride comes before a fall, and within a few months they had started to sag. What they don't tell you is that implants weigh, and once you pass fifty your skin loses its elasticity. Gravity takes over and they sag. I was not happy, so I went to see another plastic surgeon.

Ah well, he said. In his view I should have had silicone, not saline, and the implants needed to go behind the muscle, not in front. But it wasn't too late. He could do it for me. Not a problem.

Ozzy didn't want me to have them done. He'd had enough

of me mucking around with my body and he is terrified of general anaesthetics. But it's like everything else about me. Whatever I have, I hate. It wouldn't take more than a couple of days and nobody would notice, I thought, and at the same time I'd have liposuction on the bits I had never got round to doing before – my arms and my back. I booked myself in for a new breast op. It would be like a little late Christmas present from me to myself.

I needed it. I'd been having real trouble with the gastric band – acid reflux that was beyond a joke, particularly at night. It was agony. The pain would spread all across my chest and the food I had just eaten would come back up. Sometimes I would have food coming out of my nose. I was having to sleep sitting up, and during the day I couldn't stop hiccupping. My surgeon wanted to take a look as soon as I got back to LA in the New Year, so I went for a scan on 7 January.

The operation I'd had in 1999 is only given to patients who are 100 pounds over their correct weight. Obese was the word they used. Nothing is cut away: they just insert a hollow band round the upper part of your stomach. Once it's in place, and your body has recovered from the operation, they fill this band with saline solution through an access port. As the liquid expands the band, it squeezes the stomach until it's the shape of an egg-timer, creating a pouch at the top and leaving a narrow hole to connect the two parts. The result is that your stomach can only deal with a small amount of food at a time. Eat too much and it won't go down – and you feel full.

All my life my weight had gone up and down, up and down. I started dieting when I was fourteen. Every ten years a trauma would make me lose it all, and then I'd pile it back on again, and the whole business was exhausting. How you look is the emotional burden you carry around, but there's the physical burden as well. When you're large you have to wash a lot more because you smell. Just running around in the heat – as I would do every summer on tour – is like climbing a mountain. I didn't wear heels any longer because my feet couldn't take the weight. I knew people were talking about me behind my back. In planes men would avoid sitting next to me. I'd see them asking the stewards to move them. I'd have to get an extension to attach to the seat belt just to go round me. It was like a scourge, a public humiliation the whole time.

The procedure worked. From a dress size 22 I went down to a 10. At the time it seemed like a miracle, but there were downsides. First the huge amount of plastic surgery I needed to get rid of the skin that was now hanging off me. When I think of it now I can't imagine how I had the courage to go through with it. I had my tummy tucked, legs lifted, arse lifted, breasts lifted, liposuction everywhere to get rid of the fat that wouldn't shift, and I had a face lift, including my neck.

The other downside was acid reflux. Once you've had the procedure they advise you not to eat too close to bedtime. But in our family the idea of eating at seven o'clock is ridiculous. Ozzy eats late and always has done. Performers are like that – it's how they operate. So what was I supposed to do? Correct. I ate late and suffered the consequences, which was this terrible acid reflux throughout the night. Yes, I had medication but it never really worked. What I needed to do was change my attitude to food.

The reason I'd got fat in the first place was because all of my life I had eaten the wrong things, stuffed myself with pizzas, chocolate, ice cream, milk shakes, burgers, hot dogs. Just crap. I'd never bothered to wait for meals. I'd snack all the time, and then eat a meal as well. Barely thirty minutes would go by without my shovelling something down my throat. Being on the road so much of the time didn't help. Living on the run, you grab food when you can. A plate of fries here, a Danish pastry there and a Coke to wash it down.

Of course, I started out with good intentions. The pouch mustn't be allowed to overfill. You are meant to eat tiny amounts of food regularly throughout the day, such as every two hours, but literally a cupful, no more. What they're talking about is things like soup, or mashed potatoes, or vegetable purée. They like everything to be done in the blender, but you're allowed small amounts of chicken or fish as long as you chew each mouthful about a hundred times before swallowing. Oh, and no fizzy drinks and no alcohol.

For two months I tried, and then as usual my self-destructive streak kicked in. You think: one chip won't matter. You start to cheat. They tell you that a glass of wine will help relax your stomach and get more food down. So you start with that . . .

Eating for me has always been a comfort thing. If I was unhappy I would eat, and the fatter I got, the unhappier I got, so I'd go eat some more. The truth is that after forty years I wasn't about to change. I would take it to the limit and eat and eat, and when I couldn't get more food down, I'd go to the toilet, throw up, then come back and carry on eating. I could throw up three or four times a day, easy. It wasn't like being sick in the conventional sense – none of that gut-wrenching pain when you throw up from your stomach, because the food never gets that far. The band has kept it in the pouch and all that's happened is that it's backed up, down your oesophagus. It's a log jam: it can't get through the small hole down to your lower stomach where the digestion happens, so it comes back up.

You always think you can bend the rules and make it work for you. I mean, one chip? I can shit it out in the morning and I'll be fine. I had it down to an art. I could eat, make some excuse and go to the bathroom and up it would come. Initially I would get the feeling like anyone does at the back of the throat: I have to throw up, it has to come out. So you stick your fingers down, and it comes out. But over the years I wouldn't need to use my fingers. I'd just open my throat and out it would fly. I would then go back, smile and carry on eating. Like the Romans. For them: larks' tongues. Me: another helping of fries.

Everyone in the family knew what was happening. There we would be, having dinner, discussing the day's events, what so and so had done, what so and so had said, and I'd put down my napkin, say excuse me and disappear upstairs. Conversation would stop, and when I came down I could see the look on their faces. Not distaste, not anger. Anguish. The kids hated it, Ozzy hated it. The people around us hated it. It was the terrible taboo nobody talked about.

The great thing about the gastric band, as compared to other, more invasive forms of surgical stomach reduction, is that it doesn't involve cutting anything away, so it's completely reversible. The idea is that when your body has trained itself to eat less, the band can be removed. The kids were always on at me to have it taken off. They were like, 'Mum, you must take it off. We just can't stand it.' They didn't care if I put on more weight – that, after all, was the mum they grew up with, the warm, cuddly person. Nor did Ozzy. He has always said he loves me whatever size I am, and he has proved it. He loved me when I was the size of a garden shed.

The problem was me. I like being thin. I like being able to wear gorgeous clothes. I like having the energy to cope with the insane life I find myself living. I like it when somebody says, 'Hey, Sharon, you look beautiful!' I like having a career of my own, and never in a million years would I be fronting television shows if I was a dress size 20. It would not happen.

After spending Christmas and the New Year in England, we flew back to Los Angeles and an appointment with my surgeon at Cedars-Sinai hospital. Arriving back in Los Angeles in January is always a relief. Much as I love spending Christmas and the New Year in London, the joys of an English winter very quickly wear thin. California may not be the Caribbean, but it's sunny and warm and there's colour everywhere.

This time, however, I barely noticed – I was in too much pain from the acid reflux. When I got to the hospital they gave me a barium meal – I had to swallow some white stuff that would show up on a scan. The good news, they said, was that the reason wasn't pathological: there was no cancer or anything like that – it was simply that the band had slipped, something that happens, they said, in 3 per cent of cases following the procedure. The bad news was that it had caused severe inflammation. My stomach was distended and swollen: the top part, the 'pouch', was now so big it had flopped over the band, while the acid in the lower part was beginning to migrate into my intestines.

The worst was yet to come. 'There's no way we can do anything with your stomach in this condition. You have to change your diet to get the swelling down before we can operate to remove or replace the band.' If I didn't, they said, it could burst, and if that happened I could die. In the meantime they prescribed me some new medication for the acid reflux, called Nexium, designed to calm down the acid in your stomach. Or that's what it says on the bottle.

So I tried. I really did try.

Next up was the operation on 13 February to lift my sagging breasts and at the same time get rid of the chicken wings at the tops of my arms and the fat that hadn't shifted on my back. It wouldn't mean I could wear things without sleeves, but at least I'd fit into jackets without getting stuck or splitting the seams.

From the moment I came round I was in agony. The worst thing was my back. I felt as if I'd been knocked down by a bus. Then, when that seemed to have calmed down, I picked up an infection in my right breast. Where the stitches had been put in, the wound refused to heal. I was going back to the hospital every day to have it checked and was on massive doses of antibiotics. It got so bad that at one point they thought they were going to have to take the implants out. In the end they put a drain in, presumably to suck out all the pus.

No one had done anything wrong, but you are warned that there is always a huge risk of infection with cosmetic surgery. On the previous occasions I'd been lucky. This time not, and somewhere along the line I'd picked something up.

So, was it worth it? Did I end up with tits that were neat and perky and elegant? The fuck I did. Although they were higher, the business of putting the implants behind the muscle rather than in front had made them look bigger. I often couldn't squash them into my bra, or if I did manage to at least do that, they'd suddenly pop out under my arms.

For several days immediately after the operation I lay there in agony wondering, What am I doing? What is the point of all this? What am I chasing? Eternal youth? Perfection? It doesn't exist. The reality is that after the age of fifty your skin sags. You can come out of the operating theatre with the perfect breast and twelve months later it will sag, and nothing will change that. It will only get worse.

What I want to achieve is impossible. It's not that you want to be six foot tall, but you want your breasts in the right place, you want your belly button in the right place, you want your crotch in the right place. It's just that those things don't happen after a certain age. It's nothing to do with exercise either: work out, don't work out, the end result is the same, and you have to accept it. You just have to learn to be comfortable with who you are. If somebody's got a big nose and wants it changed, that's different. That's a minor thing to have done these days. But having your legs lifted, your stomach lifted, that's major fucking surgery.

I knew I shouldn't be doing it. Ever since my boobs had started to sag in the autumn I'd had this conversation with myself, in the small hours of the night. Should I, shouldn't I? As for the kids, I didn't even mention what I was going to do, as I knew what they'd say. 'Don't do it, Mum. You're insane. You're becoming a bore.' I was ashamed even to mention to it them. Their tolerance with me is done. So there I was in agony and I had to keep it to myself. I couldn't complain at the pain because it was self-inflicted. I'd brought it entirely on myself. But they all knew. They're like, 'Mum, we know.' They know my bullshit, they know what I'm doing. They knew that whatever I was saying, it was a fib anyway. I couldn't even ask them to turn the TV down. I was in absolute agony and I couldn't even ask them to get me a glass of water. All I could manage was, 'I don't feel that great.'

At least the end was in sight for the terrible agony of my acid reflux. I was chucking Nexium down my throat like it was milk shake. They were still not prepared to operate to remove the band; the swelling hadn't subsided enough. In the end they put me on a soup diet. I had to stay on it, they said, until after the operation.

Day after day, our chef David made me delicious soups: pea and mint, Jerusalem artichoke and chive, spinach – spinach they told me was particularly good. Most of them didn't even have names – David made them up as he went along. The rule was six ounces of soup every four hours and they had to be very low in sodium. I would take them in a thermos flask to wherever I was working. No fizzy drinks, no Coke, no champagne, no Perrier, not even fruit juice. I couldn't even have a large glass of water, it had to be sips. There was a vanilla protein drink I was allowed. On its own it tasted disgusting, so David would liquidise a banana into it. Over the next two and a half months I lost fifteen pounds.

One of the things that kept me from sinking into the most terrible depression was that I'd been asked to do *Dancing with the Stars*, the American spin-off of *Strictly Come Dancing*. Not as a judge, but as a contestant, and I was really looking forward to it.

I come from a long line of dancers – both my mother and her mother were professional dancers, the kind that did high kicks and wore feathers – and everyone assumed I'd end up one too. But although I spent five years at stage school, I was basically lazy, and dancing is tough, physically demanding and requires incredible commitment, which I singularly lacked. It also didn't help that I was short and dumpy.

I absolutely loved the show and was determined to go as far as I could – I am a competitive person once I get started – but I knew that to have any hope of going the distance I needed to be fit. A lot of this was pride. I wanted to go in there and for it to be like: 'Wow! AND she can dance – and just look how fit she is!'

Rehearsals were due to start in mid-March. I had just over two months to get fit, and have the operation, so there was no time to lose. After Jack moved out of the house on Doheny Road we had turned his old room into a gym for Ozzy, and this became my dance studio. I arranged for two professional dancers to come to the house and start training. We began slowly, as you have to: the warm-up exercises, the stretches and limbering up, and only then the dancing. By this time I had my date for the operation and everything was on track.

Soon my body started complaining. The truth was I was feeling like shit. I kept up my exercise programme for two weeks but all too often I'd be saying to the guys, 'Look, I'm a bit knackered today,' and I knew they were rolling their eyes and thinking: The bitch thinks she can just go in there and do it standing on her head. She can't.

I was loving it, but at the same time I was in such discomfort. My body was aching and I would get terrible stomach cramps. I was always hungry.

When I went to the doctors for one of my monthly check-ups, they were shocked at the state of me.

'What are you doing, Sharon?'

'Oh, you know. Just working out every day.'

'You have to stop! Leave your stomach muscles alone! Leave everything alone until you've had surgery. Keep drinking the soup and the water and stop this nonsense immediately. After the operation you'll be fine.'

I pulled out of *Dancing with the Stars* three weeks before rehearsals began. I told the production company that I had to work on Ozzy's new record and I couldn't do both, which was true. What was I doing even thinking about it when Ozzy had a new record coming out? My health was never mentioned. You start rumours, and the next thing you know they're nailing down your coffin. That's show business. Nobody would even think of giving you a job.

I was really pissed off that I couldn't do the show. I had been looking forward to having fun and it was a chance to get myself back on American television. But once again I'd pushed my body too far. Fat, thin, fat, thin. Exercise, no exercise. This was a war that had been going on for years – since I was a kid. After all these years of abuse it didn't know what

31

was going on any more, and it just couldn't take the punishment this time.

When I first began thinking about getting the gastric band removed a few years before, I had realised that I needed to look seriously at my eating problems if I wasn't just going to turn into a fat-arse again. For two years I tried therapy, but I kept cancelling sessions. I would make appointments and then I wouldn't turn up, either because I couldn't face what the therapist was going to tell me, or what I was going to tell her myself. It's all part of the illness.

But I didn't need therapy to tell me what the problem was. For a long time I used my weight as a shield. When I was working for Don in the seventies, before Ozzy and I fell in love and got married, I had no confidence, I didn't know who I was. I hated the role I was playing. I hated myself, from my hair to my feet – there wasn't one thing I liked about myself or my body. My weight was like a safety net. No guy would ever be interested in me if I was fat. They wouldn't want to get close – and I didn't want them to. Get too close to someone and you get hurt. This way I would never have to go through all that bullshit. And it worked for a long time. Until I fell in love with Ozzy, and he didn't care what size I was. He loved me anyway.

Then in the eighties and nineties I transformed myself again, and the weight piled on even more. I wanted to look like an English country housewife. That's what I was, after all. I was a mother, I lived in the country, and that's what I wanted the world to see me as. I knew what some of the neighbours thought – she's married to that wild man of rock who eats animals. That crazy drug addict. Not just the neighbours – anybody who didn't know me, hadn't met me. They would have this perception – Ozzy Osbourne's wife! I must have big hair and ride a motorbike and wear leather. Carry a whip. And then I would walk in, this short, dumpy little thing wearing my Laura Ashley dress and flat shoes and it was, 'You've got to be joking.' It threw people, it kept them guessing. And I liked that. It was another way of saying, 'You don't know me; you haven't got to me.' Like many people with weight issues, it was all about control.

On 30 March 2007 I finally went into Cedars-Sinai to have the operation to remove the gastric band. I had spent nearly five months on a diet of mush. If I had always eaten that way – vegetables, small amounts of food – I would never have got myself into this ridiculous situation in the first place.

As for the operation, the one they said was simple: it wasn't. I was in theatre for nearly five hours and when I came round I felt terrible. Far, far worse than I had ever felt before. When I first had it done in 1999, I was out in two days. This time they told me it would be four. In the end it took six days before I was able to go home.

Ozzy didn't visit me. He hates hospitals. Just can't cope, and Aimee is the same. The timing was good, though. Ozzy's eldest daughter Jessica and her husband Ben and their babies

Isabel and Harry were over on holiday, so they all went to stay at the house in Malibu.

Kelly came and sat by her old mother all the time. I was scared to sleep, convinced that I was going to die. No one had put that thought in my head; it came all on its own. Through guilt. The guilt of knowing I had brought this all on myself. How different the situation is with Jack. He had been flabby, some would even say fat. Liked his food and ate too much. Not any more. Nothing to do with cosmetic surgery, but by finding something that gave his life real meaning, he changed it from the bottom up. He's done it by himself with hard work, by keeping fit and treating his body with respect.

Although it took me a long time to recover, the operation was ultimately successful. They put on a new band. One part of me hopes I'll find the will power to eat properly and not need it. The other part knows that I'll just go back to the same old habits.

For two weeks after surgery you stay on liquids because your body needs to recover from the operation. Then gradually the liquids are allowed to get thicker. It felt like eating baby food. Finally, after a month, I was allowed the real thing. The real thing cut into small pieces, that is.

They give you a huge list of dos and don'ts. Mostly don'ts. No carbonated drinks. No pasta. No cakes, no bread. Crackers are fine. This time I am trying to stick to it. Now I know what happens if I don't. But who am I bullshitting? Give me a few months and I'll be packing the shit back in again. The other day I was walking round Harrods and I bought a bar of chocolate. Why did I do that? Chocolate is ludicrous. It is the worst. While I'm eating I don't savour it, I don't think: Oh, this is really great. In fact, the opposite. Immediately I don't feel great because I know what I've done. I feel guilt. So why, when I know all this, did I do it? Not content with that, I stopped and had a milk shake. Couldn't I just have had a cup of camomile tea? Of course I could. But I'm weak, which is why I think that eventually I'll get them to put the saline back in the band and make it physically impossible for me to eat the junk I do.

I stuck to the soup diet for all those months because I was feeling so sick, both before the operation and after. It was easy. Now I'm feeling fine again, my stomach's not swollen any more and I've got no reflux, and nothing comes down my nose. No little crumbs, no major bits of food that get trapped, and you end up snorting to try to keep the airways clear just to breathe. So I eat. Basically I'm a fucking glutton.

Oh, I can diet. I could diet for England. But it's like people who give up smoking. Yes, they say, giving up smoking is easy, I've done it dozens of times. I've also tried hypnosis, but I felt very weird about that. Proper therapy is the only answer, and that scares me shitless.

The logical side of my brain says that if I have the band blown up I will have acid reflux within a month. I also know that if I had an illness that was really dangerous – life-threatening – I would start eating sensibly.

I've come to realise that no matter how much money you

have, or whatever you do with the surgery, there are no short cuts for anything. They're temporary. They're only humps in the road to slow you down. You think, if I go and have my arse sucked I'll be skinny. Skinny for a few months, and then it goes straight back on.

Everything I have done to my body has been self-abuse: the eating, the dieting, the gastric band, the cosmetic surgery. Everything. You want your body to look good, but you overeat, so then you diet, and then it's hanging loose, so you have it cut off, so then you're fine, but then it starts to droop, so, Oh well, you think, I'll lift it. You put Botox in, but even Botox doesn't last for ever.

And then I look at the other side. The girls with anorexia who often end up dying of a heart attack or liver failure. Young girls these days don't give themselves time to grow into their bodies. Puppy fat, that's what it was called when I was growing up, and nobody had anorexia that I knew.

It seems to me that we've reached this ludicrous situation where so many older women – beautiful women in their forties and fifties – are trying desperately to look like they're in their twenties. Meanwhile, all the young girls are dressing like their mothers. None of it makes sense.

The emphasis on bodies now is just insane. Take Sharon Stone. A beautiful woman of nearly fifty who has – naturally – the body of a twenty-year-old. Recently there was a picture of her in a magazine in a swimsuit, diving into a pool, and they'd circled cellulite. Why?

The paparazzi-driven magazines you get nowadays all suggest it's abnormal to look like a normal, healthy young woman. As for the clothes they wear: footballers' wives, all of thirteen years of age, walking around with Hermès handbags and old women's clothes, ridiculous evening dresses, backless, split up to their arse. I want to ask them: Why are you doing that? Why would you want to do that? When my friends and I were that age, the last thing we would wear was what our mothers were wearing. They are now wearing clothes that would be more appropriate on a woman in her forties.

And the jewellery – you need to be a woman to wear a big stone. It doesn't look real on a younger girl. The WAG generation buy these things because they're expensive, because it shows they have money, but they don't wear it well because they're too young. As for the American girls, the Olsen twins, Nicole Richie, Paris Hilton – the make-up, the hair extensions – they all look like Vegas hookers to me.

I feel like telling these young women: wear your suntan, a little bit of lip-gloss, nothing more. You look ridiculous with that silly handbag and that great big watch on. Half the time they look like they're off to a fancy-dress party.

You look at them and you think: What are you doing? Wear a pair of jeans and some tennis shoes. Think of Audrey Hepburn. She would wear a little pair of cut-off black trousers, a white shirt and big sunglasses and she would look like a million dollars.

We all want to stand out from the crowd, but to do that

you have to have an individual sense of style. Yet these girls all have the same dress on. They've all been to the same stylist. How many times in these magazines do you see a heading: Who wore it better? This one or that one?

Sometimes I'll be in Bond Street or somewhere like that and the phone will go and it'll be Gary, my publicist. When I'm in London he always knows where I am, because the paps or a paper will call him and say, 'Sharon's in Bond Street, what's she doing there?' So he'll call me and go, 'Have you got your make-up on?' And I'm like, 'Fuck off, Gary! I don't care. I couldn't give a shit. I'm not Posh, I'm not Elizabeth Hurley. I'm a fifty-five-year-old woman.' What I look like is not my trademark, so I couldn't care less. I do like to present myself well, but if I'm going out shopping I'm not going to put the full slap on and be coordinated.

There's so much pressure to look a certain way. Young, thin, big tits. But ultimately it doesn't make you happy. We try so hard to be perfect. Our bodies have to be perfect; we have to speak perfectly. It's so fucking boring! I spent years punishing my body because I hated myself. Nowadays I feel better about myself – there was no great revelation, just a combination of age and experience. A dawning realisation that I didn't have to go on playing those roles – the dutiful daughter, the respectable housewife. Don't imagine the war is over. I'm still fighting my body, still abusing it when I don't eat properly. But I'm starting to realise that any changes you make – any little victories – they're only temporary. You can only fight for so long. In the end, what happens to your body is out of your control. My father's illness has shown me that. I don't know if that's frightening or if it's a relief. Because fighting yourself gets tiring. In the end you're gonna lose, so what's the point?

Everywhere you look now, it's all about anti-ageing: creams, sunblock, laser treatment – but it's hard to know when to stop. What I really want is to find that quiet part in me that can grow old gracefully. I know I'm not alone. Most women of my generation struggle with this dilemma. Our youth may be behind us, but at fifty we're not the has-beens our mothers were. But where do you draw the line? My hair is a good example. I've dyed it now for more than half my life. So when do I stop? And how? What about other hair? Do I really want to strut my stuff on TV with my moustache showing? Yet I know that when I have grandchildren they'll want that cosy, comfortable person like my own nana was.

I'd like to think that I'll know when it's time to stop, but it's one thing to recognise the need, it's another to accept that the moment has arrived. Will I know when to say, That's it? Enough.

# Hollywood

The CD comes to an end, and the room falls silent. I lean over and change it, press play. Music fills the room again.

There was always so much music in the house when I was growing up. Our house was full of it: records, the radio, my father singing. He had an amazing voice and he was always passionate about music. As a young man he trained as a cantor and so could read and write music – how many rock managers can do that today?

My father taught me so much. Through him I got to see the greatest entertainers of all time perform. His love of music was so broad and he loved nothing more than sharing it. One minute I would be watching Jerry Lee Lewis on stage laying into his piano and the next I would be at the theatre watching Julie

Andrews. I mean, he started out his musical life in a synagogue in Manchester and ended up producing the Small Faces and ELO! He loved listening to opera but he could quite easily sit and listen to the Sex Pistols and appreciate what they were doing.

I was born into the entertainment industry, which I thank my parents for. But I don't think Don ever really respected me as a businesswoman. When I first worked with my father I never questioned the way he operated. I just wanted him to be pleased with me. I wanted to be needed. If you did what he wanted, then he was happy. I wanted to be the good, loyal girl – sign whatever he wanted me to sign, lie, bullshit – whatever he wanted me to do, I would do. But as I grew into my twenties I began to reject the business methods he taught me. Don came from the generation of managers who thought, I'll make you a star and you'll get all the fame, but I get all the money!

And I hated the people my father hung with. The Krays. Some fucking Italian heavies from New York, bragging about how many people they'd knocked off or crippled. My family were gangster groupies. I hated all that. And I began to distance myself from it.

The truth is that Don never accepted that I was a businesswoman in my own right. As far as he was concerned I'd stolen Ozzy from him – that was all. He never once said that he was proud of me – of what I'd achieved. And yet just a few months ago – Valentine's Day 2007 – I had been invited to a reception at Buckingham Palace to celebrate women 'who have made a significant contribution to business and industry in the United Kingdom'.

It turned into a fantastic day. When the car swept through the main gates I saw the guardsmen with those fur hats and ridiculous straps across their chins mouthing my name. Of course they're absolutely forbidden to speak, so I stuck my tongue out at them.

On these kinds of occasions it doesn't do to go overdressed; I was wearing a navy trouser suit, generally quite toned down: a lot less jewellery, a lot less cleavage, a lot less make-up. As Coco Chanel once said: 'Fashion changes, style remains.' It was OK for her, and it's OK for me.

Before we joined the main reception a few of us were invited into a comparatively small, intimate receiving room, where we could have private words with the royal family, just the women. Princess Anne was there, Camilla, Edward's wife Sophie and Birgitte, the Duchess of Gloucester, and, of course, the Queen herself.

I've been lucky enough to meet the Queen on several occasions now, and I think she's incredible. There she is, over eighty years old, and she must have been standing for over two hours. She's a very shy lady, so if both of you say nothing, or what amounts to nothing, it can become very embarrassing. I mean, if you say, 'How are you?' what's she going to say? 'Oh, actually I'm not at all well, I've got the shits, and my feet are killing me.'

Dog owners are always happy to talk about their dogs, particularly if they go in for it seriously, which the Queen does. So I asked her how the doggies were doing. There was a horrible accident a couple of years back when two of Princess Anne's dogs – English bull terriers – killed one of the Queen's corgis during a romp in Windsor Great Park, so we talked about that, and then she was telling me about how she was looking after her granddaughter Zara's dog – because Zara was away doing horse business. (Another fail-safe topic for grandmothers is talking about their grandchildren.)

After this private chat, we joined the other two hundred or so guests in a huge reception room for drinks and canapés. There were some amazing women there, though I only got to talk to a few of them. There were dress designers, stage designers, inventors, the woman who started up Rigby & Peller, who has been making bras for the Queen since 1960. I met a young woman who had just invented a new board game; handbag-maker Anya Hindmarch; interior designer Kelly Hoppen; former journalist Josephine Fairley, who created Green & Black organic chocolate; Sarah Doukas of Storm, Kate Moss's agent; Karren Brady, who runs Birmingham City football team, Jacqueline Gold, who started up the Ann Summers sex-shop chain – as long as you were a successful businesswoman who had done something on your own, then you had the chance to be invited. I'd only met Karren Brady before, but everyone was so friendly. Gradually, after about a couple of hours, the royal family disappeared and the footmen began saying, 'This way out, ladies.' A group of us were so busy chatting that we didn't notice everybody else had gone. Not even the footmen seemed to care, and they kept bringing us out more goodies to eat.

Then I did something I never do.

It turned out that the ladies I was with had arranged to have lunch afterwards, and they invited me to go with them. And I actually went. Normally I would never have gone out to a ladies' lunch on a work day, which this was. But I just thought: Fuck it. Ozzy was in LA. Even Minnie was in LA. Nobody was expecting me anywhere. I had no meetings. So I went. I felt like a kid, I felt like I was skiving.

We met up at an Italian restaurant off Bond Street. Sarah Doukas, Kelly Hoppen, Anya Hindmarch, Josephine Fairley and me. We didn't roll out till after five o'clock. For me there was no wine, not much in the way of food (still on my diet of mush), but I wouldn't have missed it for the world. I loved it, and I made some new friends.

I was just coming back from the bathroom, before we left, when a lady stopped me and asked for a table for two. So I showed her to a table. That's what comes of not wearing enough jewellery and a navy blue suit.

I'd had so much fun. It was great to spend time with all these smart, funny women, who had achieved so much success, and on their own terms. And with my wall-to-wall schedules, I rarely get the chance to do anything off the cuff. I'm not a girly girl, and I don't do girly lunches – which is how I would have thought of it if I'd walked past and seen this group of smartly dressed women sitting in a Bond Street restaurant late into the afternoon.

Don would never have understood a lunch like that. You didn't do anything unless it was directly for the business. But he was operating in a tough industry. Tough then and tough now. And although I didn't approve of Don's methods, he did teach me how to stand up for myself. And as a woman in the music business, believe me, you have to fight every step of the way.

# 2

## Show Business

Ozzfest is a touring festival that travels around America for about six weeks in the summer. I started it in 1996 when I couldn't find a suitable tour for Ozzy to play on. I could never have imagined when I had the idea that we'd still be going into the next century.

It's run entirely by me and my team. Most years we average about twenty-one bands. Ozzy always headlines, and I try to get a mix of established names and newcomers to give the fans a good day out. It starts at nine-thirty in the morning and ends somewhere around ten in the evening – over twelve hours of non-stop hard-edge music. But, like everybody else, I have to work with the material available. Agents play their own games: you can have X as long as you have Y. All that shit. Deals have to be cut and it can be a snake pit. But that's business.

Until very recently Black Sabbath – the original line-up of Ozzy, Tony Iommi, Bill Ward and Geezer (Terry) Butler – always played before Ozzy did the final set of the night with his own band. Although the feud between Ozzy and Sabbath lasted for years, it is now long over and Ozzfest is an opportunity for us all, band members, wives and children, to spend a few weeks together on the road, in our buses, catching up on news, watching the children grow up – the usual stuff of families, which is what it feels like. Although it's hard work putting it all together, it's a well-oiled machine and it's worth it. Surrounded by his fans and old friends, and doing what he does best, Ozzy is in his element. However, some things you can't control.

Clear Channel (now called Live Nation) are major players in the entertainment industry: they own 1,100 radio stations, plus thirty television stations, billboards and most of the theatres on Broadway. They put on musicals, skateboarding events, motocross, stock-car racing: you name it, they do it. Most importantly for us, they own the majority of what in America are called 'sheds', and what in England are called arenas and amphitheatres. In addition, they own every major venue in Europe. They are as close to a monopoly as it gets without offending the government bodies that oversee such things.

Clear Channel's dominance over the last ten years has changed the way the music industry works. In the old days, if you didn't like the deal you were being offered, you could go to another promoter. Now every promoter works for Clear Channel. Other than in Chicago, where there are still independent promoters, Clear Channel is the only game in town. Where once it was hoods running the industry, now it is run by corporations and Christian fundamentalists based in Texas, major supporters of G. W. Bush.

There's no bartering. You either accept the offer or you go away.

Three years into Ozzfest, we signed with Clear Channel and stayed with them for five. They gave us good money, but at the same time it's not just about money with me. It's no secret that I don't like their tactics. The venues are often in full sun, yet no shade is provided. Kids are not allowed to take in their own water. Water is for sale. It's the same with food. The fans can eat and drink all they want all day long, but they can only buy from Clear Channel. That – and the parking – is how they make their money.

In the spring of 2005 I was putting together the line-up for that summer's Ozzfest. We had decided we'd like Velvet Revolver as Ozzy's major support band. Slash, their lead guitar player, is a good friend of Ozzy's and mine.

Clear Channel had other ideas. They wanted Velvet Revolver on another tour and so they weren't available for us, but the English heavy metal band Iron Maiden was. Iron Maiden's agents were CAA, the same as ours, and they saw Ozzfest as an opportunity to break them in America. Not only did they insist we have them, but they insisted we paid them. It got worse. CAA also represented four other bands on that year's Ozzfest and I later discovered they had signed a 'favoured-nation' deal with Clear Channel, which meant that each of these bands was getting paid the same amount of money, far in excess of what they were worth, and which we ultimately paid for.

Ozzy was not happy. Neither was I. The name Iron Maiden comes from a torture device used in the middle ages, and that just about sums them up. I have always felt they were very second-division with no musical credibility. The idea that we were going to have them on Ozzfest made me fear for Ozzy's sobriety, which, only a year in, seemed so fragile.

I knew we were going to have trouble early on when, months before the tour opened, Iron Maiden began insisting on this and that for their set: pyro, complicated lighting and the rest of it. They would be the last act on the main stage before Black Sabbath went on, and I was not prepared to compromise on Sabbath's stage set to satisfy these wankers. At first I hoped they would pull out of the deal of their own accord, which would have suited me very well. Even if we sold fewer tickets, at least I wouldn't have to pay them the extortionate amount of money they were getting, and I could get lesser-known bands to fill the time slot. I told our stage manager: 'I want to build the biggest, ugliest fucking set so they can't get a feather on stage, and they can shove it up their arse. Perhaps then they'll fuck off.'

They didn't. They knew that Ozzfest was a great gig for them, and so a compromise was reached in terms of their demands, but I knew the fuse was still smouldering.

Iron Maiden are the cliché eighties heavy metal band. Very English. While they do have a fan base in America, it's nothing like their huge profile in England and Europe. And I understand how hard it must be for a band that are used to headlining to find themselves, at their age, as a support. But, hey, that's business. That's what they signed up for.

Visually they are pure Spinal Tap: tight blue jeans, ridiculously long bleached hair and pristine white trainers, which they obviously have brand new every day. Bruce Dickinson, their lead singer, likes to put himself a little apart. Although he has the same working-class roots as Ozzy, for some reason he ended up at an English boarding school. He prides himself on his sword-fencing ability and pilots himself about in his own plane. He's basically a bit of a prat. The rest of the band are pretty all-right guys, good musicians with a great sense of humour. Family guys, and I like them.

So that was the position when we started the tour in July 2005. Ozzy's not happy, I'm pissed off because I think that CAA has forced us into this. However, there's nothing to be done and I decide I'll just have to make the best of it. After all, we've never been friendly and it's not like we hang out in each other's dressing rooms. I'll stay clear, and as far as Ozzy is concerned, he never arrives at the venue more than an hour before he goes on, so they'll already be on stage by the time he gets there. He won't have to see them.

So the first day they go on stage, and immediately the singer starts complaining about the sound system to the crowd.

'When we come back here,' he yells, 'we'll have a proper sound system so you can all hear us and you'll know what we're really like.' Then, in the middle of his set, he has another go – this time about how he's not one of these bands that's sold out to MTV – a blatant reference to Ozzy and *The Osbournes*.

So OK, bad day, first day of the tour, everybody's getting settled. Fine. Then it happens again: the second show, and the third, the fourth, the fifth. Worse shit. Every day it gets worse. I do nothing. I never have eye contact with him; I hear nothing through the management. Just these bitchfests every night from the stage. No official complaints. Am I surprised? No. From us, they're getting $185,000 a show. On off days they do their own show in different cities along the Ozzfest trail and play to half-empty houses. They could leave at any time they want and I'd say: 'God bless. Go. Take the iron maiden and fuck off home.'

Meanwhile, the other bands and the crew are getting more and more irate. Because he just doesn't stop. And it's boring. Then the ageing twat decides to spice things up with a personal attack about Ozzy having a teleprompter. Now Ozzy has a teleprompter because he doesn't do the same set every night. Ozzy has the kind of voice that takes no prisoners, and if he's been overdoing it and the voice isn't good, he'll drop some songs and put in others. My husband never knows how his voice will be from show to show, and in terms of alternative songs, he's spoiled for choice with forty years of work to pull from, and they're all there on the computer. He'll suddenly say to the guys mid-set, OK, we'll do a song from the second album, called X, and it'll come up on the monitors on stage, and the lyrics will be there. He might not have sung it in a year or two or four. So slimeball Dickinson bangs on about that. And it's just ridiculous. Yes, the lyrics come up on the monitor, but as anyone that has watched Ozzy perform knows perfectly well, he's too busy leaping round the stage and throwing buckets of water over the fans to go near the monitors, let alone read them. Plus he's severely dyslexic. The idea of Ozzy staring at the monitor and reading lyrics that he wrote himself is just ridiculous. It's a safety net for everyone involved.

Every night we get this rant. And every night it gets more and more personal, scathing attacks on Ozzy and also Ozzfest itself, which amounts to an attack on me, though never by name. What I also know is that the singer has never even seen Ozzy on this tour, not him personally, not the act.

What Iron Maiden don't know, because they have never played Ozzfest before, is that the crew on Ozzfest is like a family. We travel together, play together, eat together. The same guys come back year after year, and an attack on Ozzy is an attack on them. So everybody around me is going, 'Whatja going to do, whatja going to do?' 'Nothing,' I tell them. 'Let it carry on. Do nothing. There will be a payback.' The only thing I insisted on was that Ozzy never knew. Not a word was to reach him of Iron Maiden's disrespectful behaviour.

So we get to Los Angeles, the Devore Stadium at San Bernardino, about two hours east of LA, almost halfway to Palm Springs. It's a beautiful place, quite high, set in a national park surrounded by tree-covered hills. It's a natural bowl, with the lawn – the non-seated area – rising on a hill above the stage. Now this is a big LA show. The place can hold up to 50,000 people and Iron Maiden haven't played in LA for probably six or seven years. Together with New York, Los Angeles is the big one. So I get some friends of mine, lots of the crew guys, and tell them what I have in mind. No press gang – this is volunteers only, and there are plenty of them, fifty to be exact. It's the end of the tour and we've put up with this shit for twenty-seven performances across America and there is no way on God's earth I am going to let this prick walk away without some retaliation.

Ozzy still knows nothing about it. Not the fact that they've been attacking him personally, nor that I have plans of my own to even up the score. It is totally me.

I've had six weeks to plan my revenge, and I get it. I order in about fifty trays of eggs and several catering-size jars of peanut butter. The eggs we leave intact. The peanut butter gets scooped out and mixed with water until it's good and gluggy. Then we do the same with a few industrial tins of baked beans. And I get some ice-cubes for the final touch. I've done something like this once before, years ago, with a nanny who misbehaved and needed to be taught a lesson. My instructions to the guys are simple: 'When Iron Maiden come out,' I say, 'pelt the singer. Forget the other guys. During the first minute of the set you just pelt that little fucker. He wants to play? Let's play.' So these fifty guys are at the front ready with their ammunition when Iron Maiden come on.

The singer opens his mouth and their arms go out and my God did they pelt him: eggs breaking on his face, baked beans in his hair, ice-cubes sliding all over the stage. The little fucker was obviously shocked to shit. He didn't know what the hell was happening. Meanwhile I stood in the wings, my arms folded, and I gloated. But it wasn't over yet. By this time adrenalin was pumping through me. He'd been complaining about the sound system – a sound system that worked perfectly well and that nobody else had complained about – so I thought: I'll give you something to complain about, you little shit. I'll show you! Stage left, right by the mixing desks, there's a huge steel lever about two feet long that controls all the sound electrics. The master switch. I walked over, reached up and pulled the fucker down. Totally on the spur of the moment, but oh, how gratifying: the sound died. One moment he was wailing, next moment nothing. No sound from him, no sound from the band. Amps off, mike off. Silence. After a few seconds I pushed the lever up again and the sound came back on. The audience had no idea what was happening, neither did the little fucker prancing round on the stage – it could have been a genuine glitch, a technical fault in the PA. He couldn't see me, blinded by the lights, which weren't affected. So to show who was boss, I threw it again on the next song. And the next. I'd show him what bad sound really was.

When he came off I said, 'Now just fuck off.'

I felt bad for the rest of the band. The rest of the band were good guys and would never say a word against Ozzy. They knew their singer was a big-mouthed prat. In Europe, Iron Maiden are a bigger draw than Ozzy. They play to more people and sell more albums. But in America, both north and south, and in Japan – the biggest markets for this genre of music – they don't come near. The one thing that Ozzy has over Iron Maiden is musical credibility, and I think the singer knows it. No matter how long he sings, he will never attain either Ozzy's musical credibility or the levels of adulation Ozzy gets. I can only think it was all about jealousy. Pure and simple.

I have no regrets. I just thought: Twenty-seven shows you've been a pig, and it serves you right. In all the weeks of the tour I never once spoke to him. Nor he to me. Not a word. Their manager knew exactly what they were doing and I'd have bloody egged him too if he'd come close to me, but he wasn't that much of an idiot. If he had, I'd have told him, 'You know what? You don't take somebody's money and slag them. If you don't like it, then fuck off. Leave. You think you can do it on your own? Then go out and do it on your own.' They knew they couldn't. They needed Ozzfest, which is why they stayed. As it was, they got more publicity because of the egging than they ever got through playing. Unfortunately, the other guys in the band had to suffer. The bass player, who was a gentleman, had already apologised to Ozzy. This was before the egging, so Ozzy had no idea what he was talking about. Throughout the tour he never knew they were bad-mouthing him. I made sure of that, because he would have been absolutely destroyed. The first Ozzy knew about any of it was because of the eggs – the stage had to be hosed down before Sabbath went on.

In retrospect, I should have told them to fuck off after the first night.

After the Iron Maiden fiasco, we decided to leave our agents, CAA. Rob Light – the head of the music division – had represented Ozzy for ten years by then, and CAA had made a fortune from him. Not only had Ozzy been constantly touring, but Rob Light had been able to use Ozzfest to break many of his other bands.

If I had any second thoughts after such a long association, they were dispelled after the chance discovery of an email Rob sent to Clear Channel. Email is a great boon, but it can very easily go wrong. Rob Light was sending it to Michael Rapino at Clear Channel, but Rob's assistant sent it to Michael Guarracino at my office, with devastating results for them.

Unfortunately I can't reproduce Rob's email here, but it centred around whether Iron Maiden were responsible for some disappointing ticket sales. Clear Channel had wondered whether Iron Maiden had not been worth what they were paid, and weren't pulling in the crowds. Rob was quick to leap to Iron Maiden's defence – at our expense. He suggested that it had more to do with Ozzy moving dates around, and the other bands – even that perhaps Ozzfest itself was 'tired'. He went on to shower praise on Iron Maiden for being 'good participants in the tour', which, given their lead singer's behaviour towards Ozzy, made no sense to me. By defending Iron Maiden so vigorously, Rob must have known that any blame would automatically switch to Ozzy and me. After years of working together, I was furious – more for Ozzy than for myself. So I sent the following response:

Rob,

Regarding your email to Jane Holman that you cc'd Michael Guarracino on, even though I already told you quite clearly on Saturday how hurt and let down I was, I feel I have to put this in writing. Rob, you are Ozzy and Black Sabbath's agent. You know we are partners with Clear Channel and are contracted for another Ozzfest tour with them. You are the man who next year is meant to go in and cut our deal with Clear Channel. Do you realize that you have put in writing to them that 'maybe the festival

(Ozzfest) is tired'? And that maybe ticket sales are soft because of Black Sabbath?

How can you hope to go in and negotiate next year with any strength after making comments like that? You should be ashamed of yourself as an agent and more importantly as a human being for not showing the proper respect for Ozzy Osbourne and Black Sabbath for what they have achieved both professionally and personally.

There were a couple of things in your e-mail to Jane that you did not address. Firstly, let's start with Iron Maiden's fee. From day one everybody addressed the issue that Iron Maiden was being overpaid. However great a band they are, and however much you are devoted to them, it still doesn't make them worth what they're being paid nightly in addition to the Clear Channel bonus that they're getting.

Yes, Ozzy and I did take your advice and believed you when you said that they were the best band for Ozzfest right now and that they would be worth the money. We believed you even though I did my research by pulling the box office receipts from their last two tours from Pollstar which told a totally different story.

Your remark that 'It's not Rick's fault or Iron Maiden's fault that Ozzy's had to move so many dates.' Rob, so many dates happens to be two. Furthermore, your comment 'the fact that Rick negotiated a deal to protect against such changes is just indication that they knew what they were dealing with.'

Rob, what does that mean? Please tell me. I hope it means that they were blessed to get a tour that allowed them to

1) be paid more than they're worth

2) receive kudos and credibility from the metal/hard rock community

3) play in front of larger crowds in the U.S. than they've played to in over 15 years.

One thing I can't take away from Iron Maiden is that they do sell a lot of t-shirts, but so do Motorhead and Black Label Society, so what does that mean?

Your comment that Iron Maiden 'have been good participants in this tour. They play on time, do a good set, get off on time.' Again, you are right, but you forgot to mention the singer's nightly tirades against Ozzfest, Ozzy and Black Sabbath, such as, 'We don't need a reality show to be credible' and 'next time we come back we'll have a decent PA system,' 'I don't need a teleprompter to remember the words to our songs' and finally 'Next time we come back we'll be playing new songs not like these guys (Black Sabbath) who play the same songs every year.'

# Show Business

I'm sure Jane Holman is big enough to take care of herself regarding your comment on the 'venom she's feeling towards Iron Maiden.' I wonder if you're a big enough man to apologize to her for such an ugly statement and to also apologize to Black Sabbath. Might I remind you Rob that I tried to call you four times on Thursday and four times on Friday. It took me eight calls to you before I could get you to call me back. It's now 12 noon on Tuesday and I've still not heard back from you regarding any rescheduling of dates or Ozzy getting any remuneration for shows he didn't play. However, one thing I do know is how much Rob Light loves Iron Maiden. Your infatuation with them seems to go far beyond just business. It seems very personal to me.

I really think you need a reality check here. Might I suggest that you take a picture of Ozzy Osbourne and a picture of Bruce Dickinson and stop a few people on the street and ask them if they know who they are.

I'm certain the response will be 'Well, that's Ozzy Osbourne, but I don't know who the other guy is.' You might even start this experiment in the lobby of the CAA building. I'm sure you'll even have trouble finding someone who can identify Bruce Dickinson there. At that point you can declare that 'He is the singer in this amazing band Iron Maiden who receives a guarantee of $185,000 a night which I negotiated for him.'

Rob, it's been 10 years since Ozzy agreed to have you represent him as his agent and we've been loyal to you ever since. We were so loyal to you that we gave CAA the negotiations for our show with MTV. It wasn't our fault that the agent at CAA totally dropped the ball and couldn't negotiate more than $10,000 an episode for the entire family. Yes, WE HAVE been loyal to you, as you certainly can't say that you've ever enticed us to stay with lavish gifts and dinners.

On closing, I just want you to know that Ozzy Osbourne is an amazing human being who is truly deserving of being called a superstar and a legend.

Sadly for him, his agent doesn't think so.

Sharon

Subsequently Rob attempted to pull back from the brink by following up my suggestion of the Ozzy/Bruce Dickinson recognisability quotient. He personally took placards with pictures of both of them out on the streets to test public reaction and sent us photos to prove it. Ozzy won hands down. But as far as our relationship with CAA was concerned, the damage was done.

It was all so sad. Frustrating. After all these years in the business I still had to fight so hard for Ozzy. This business sometimes forces me to behave in a way that I don't like, but I have to do it to protect Ozzy. This was a prime example –

CAA have made millions from Ozzy, yet behind his back they run him down. That's show business.

You can never take anything for granted. The business with CAA reminded me that even the people who are supposed to be working for you aren't always on your side. You have to watch your back the whole time.

I see these kids auditioning for the *The X-Factor* and I worry for them. These young, innocent kids with big dreams – they have no idea what they're letting themselves in for. The music business is so tough. Of course the show does its best to prepare them, but you can only protect them so much. I mean, Ozzy has forty years in the business, and it's still a fight every day. What chance do these young kids have?

One thing Ozzy does know is that I will always protect him, will always be on his side, no matter what. But not every star can marry their manager!

# Hollywood

A door slams somewhere down the corridor. I jump, but my father sits unmoving, staring into space.

I wonder what Don would have done about Iron Maiden in his heyday? He'd probably have sent a couple of heavies round. Strung that little prat of a singer up by the ankles and dangled him out of a tall building to teach him a fucking lesson.

He would have enjoyed it all; he would have thought it was fucking hilarious. Don thrived on arguments, fights. Feuds. And so did I, for many years. I was my father's daughter. I could fight with the best of them. I had a ferocious temper – I was famous for it. I learned from my father that fear is power. It definitely is. You can get people to do most of what you want through fear. People will not question you when they're afraid of you. And when I was younger I got off on that, I totally got off on that. Not any more.

When I was first with Ozzy I lived on a knife-edge and I'd have complete meltdowns. Anybody who multi-tasks like I do, high-pressure, stressful things – whoever you are – you have some sort of reaction to that: hissy fits, wobblers, whatever you want to call it. Something has to give. Then I discovered Zoloft. It's an anti-depressant. That was a long time ago, but I'm still on it. It keeps everything calm – nothing fazes me. I think it's that plus a combination of getting older. I just don't want to fight any more, not if I can help it.

With me, what I do is stuff things. I don't want to be confronted. I don't want to deal with it, so I'll just bury it. It's like stuffing things into a cupboard, and the door gets harder and harder to close. At some point that door will fly open. And once every few years it does. One of those days when the pressure's up and the telly is on extra loud, and the kids are on the phone, and Ozzy is complaining, and the dogs never stop barking and I've got the accountant waiting on the other line . . . you just break. Scream. Cry. I will get my head and just bang it, bang it against the wall. To hurt myself. Once upon a time I used to cut myself, but I've done cutting – that was years ago. Now I bang my head.

The feuds still get to me, though. For as long as I can remember, the Arden family was at war with itself. There was always one side not speaking to another. Petty arguments, people not talking for years, for reasons nobody could even remember. Both my parents played the game, even when we were just little kids. One month David would be the favourite, the next month it was Sharon. You never knew where you were. It kept you on your toes.

It was divide and rule. If you have everybody fighting one another then they can't gang up on you. You're in control. It never stopped; it just went on and on. And you had to pick a side. God help you if you were caught between two warring sides, like my niece Gina.

All her life Gina has been a piggy in the middle of our feuding family. She's like the little sister I never had. My real sister – Gina's mother Dixie – was sixteen years older than me and practically brought me up, even though she was only my half-sister. My father couldn't stand her, like he couldn't stand Richard, my half-brother. He couldn't stand either of his stepchildren. Dixie married young, and naturally my parents didn't approve – they refused to let me be her bridesmaid and refused to go to her wedding, just as they refused to let Gina be my bridesmaid. How could they stop me having Gina as my bridesmaid? Because Ozzy and I had no money at the time – Don was refusing to pay Ozzy what he owed him – so Don would have had to foot the bill to fly them to our wedding. He didn't, so that was that.

In 1982, shortly after we married, when my father set out to destroy Ozzy and me, I decided I had to break from him for ever if we were to survive, and as my mother was as deep into the hatred as he was, the split included her too. She never even saw her grandchildren. But Gina was always there for me.

It's been so difficult for her. Like any little girl, she loved her grandma and she didn't understand why my name could never be mentioned. But it was like I no longer existed. For any of them: for Dixie, for my mum, for Richard, for David, I had been wiped off the family record.

Gina knew I wasn't the ogre, the evil witch I was made out to be. When she was a little girl she would come and stay with us in Wimbledon and I would babysit her. She could only have been about eight. I remember teaching her how to put on mascara, spitting on the block and putting on layer after layer, separating each lash with a pin before giving it another coat and then another until her lashes were like fur. I taught her to swear and as she got older I would take her out to clubs – entirely inappropriate, but she loved it and I loved her.

Later, when times were hard with Ozzy, Gina was my escape route. She was living then in a little attic flat high above Piccadilly. She insisted that I took her bed while she slept on the sofa. I don't know what I would have done without her.

Gina tried to retain a relationship with her grandmother, but eventually they pushed her out. They couldn't stand it that she was still in touch with me. In the end, like me, Gina didn't even go to her grandmother's funeral. I couldn't have cared less when my mother died. I felt absolutely nothing. But Gina cared, and I know she was desperately sad. As a little girl she had adored her grandma. When she got older and Don was away in America with his mistress, she would go and stay with her to keep her company. Only much later did she realise that she was being used. That Don needed someone to take the focus away from his double life.

She used to tell me how she felt she wasn't welcome, so she took a step back. She'd describe how Dixie told her she ought to go and visit. But Gina said, 'How can I? None of them want me there and I don't want to deal with that any more. I haven't done anything wrong.' But in their eyes she had. There were no half measures. 'You're either with us or against us.' It was a game they had played over years, and Gina was just the latest in the line.

It was Don's way of saying 'I own you'. It was all about control. But he paid a huge price. All that feuding – in the end he fell out with everyone. And where did that leave him? Stuck in a room off Hollywood Boulevard with somebody who's paid to sit with him. It frightens me. I don't want to end up like that. I don't want to end up alone. My friends are so important to me – I'm so blessed. I remember when I was a kid, my parents would have so-called friends over and it would be lovely. And then they'd leave and they were 'prats' and 'cunts' and 'idiots'. And as a child I just didn't understand it. We'd just had a lovely day – where did all that come from? Half the time my dad didn't mean it – it was just a way of talking. He didn't know how to express affection. But it was always very confusing as a child.

That's why I try to avoid the arguments these days. There's another one brewing – different sides of the family arguing about where Don should be buried when he dies. The doctors don't think it will be long now. Some people want him to be buried in Manchester with his family. Others think he should be buried with my mother in Surrey. There are conflicting stories about what Don wanted, and now it's too late to ask.

I don't know what I think about it, nor do I want to think about it. I don't want the responsibility. I didn't ask for it. It's all just bullshit. I'm so tired of it all.

The only thing that really sets me off these days is if someone attacks my family. Then I'll just explode. It's something I'm often asked: how I can be so polite one minute and then so fierce the next. It's my family – I'll fight like a lioness for them. That's what mothers do, isn't it?

# 3

---

# Feuds

People fall out all the time, but when you're famous things can really blow up out of proportion. Next, it gets reported in the newspapers and suddenly you've got a feud going, and sometimes it can last for years. It's like I said before, I speak from the heart, and sometimes I say things in the heat of the moment that come back to haunt me later. But I can't regret it. It means I get into trouble sometimes, and of course if the other person is famous, then the press have a field day. There's nothing they like better than celebrity slanging matches.

I only ever really lose my temper if I think someone is attacking someone close to me, or if they pick on someone who can't answer back for themselves.

*

In November 2006 I was invited to a Prince's Trust event in the newly reopened Roundhouse in Camden, north London, called Invest in Futures. The whole thing was organised by key names in the City and the guest list was made up of hedge-fund managers and that sort of thing, people who've done extremely well for themselves over the last thirty years. There was an auction, hosted by Clive Anderson, and I was there to encourage the women in particular to open their chequebooks. Ozzy was working, so I invited Louis Walsh along as my escort.

If you'd added up the wealth in the Roundhouse that night, there would have been billions and billions, and basically my job was to say, 'Stop fucking around and give us your money.' Men approach auctions like this as a pissing contest. X has given this much, so I'll go double. That's why these auctions work. With women the approach is more complicated. 'Look, missus,' I said during my speech, pointing to some woman in a couture gown. 'Give us that two hundred quid you were going to spend on a pair of shoes next week. You'll survive. Or that Louis Vuitton handbag you've had your eye on. Just give us the five hundred quid instead, because your five hundred quid is going to change somebody's life. Not only that, you will feel better about yourself. I'm talking personally, from experience. Sometimes I think, Why am I buying something I'll probably only wear once? Why don't I write a cheque for a grand or a couple of grand or ten grand? I'll only spunk it up the wall anyway on something ridiculous I will never wear or never use. But if I give it to the Trust it will change some-one's life.'

Too often you get people at events like this that talk all this good-cause fluff. I don't see any point. Instead of getting up there and talking a load of bollocks, I try to talk to them on the level of 'That's what we're here for, stop fucking around and write us a cheque.'

At dinner I sat next to the chairman, a man called Michael Marks of NewSmith Capital. Camilla was on his other side and across from us was Prince Charles, who was sitting next to Gwyneth Paltrow. For some reason I thought she might be a bit stuck-up, but in fact she was absolutely gorgeous and down-to-earth. I realised I was just doing what I criticise other people for – being judgemental with some-one before I'd got to know them. I suppose we're all a bit guilty of that. We were also joined by Sting and his wife Trudie Styler. Sting was providing the music that night.

A few years ago, this could have been awkward to say the least. For years there was bad blood between Sting and us. In the eighties he was always running Ozzy down. Fine, we were not in the same league: totally different music, totally different audience, totally different everything, and on a personal level our paths had never crossed. But in interviews he would belit-tle Ozzy's genre of music. To some extent he was using Ozzy's name because Ozzy was the face of that music. His opinion, so fair enough. But then some time in the nineties, he went to China, or Cambodia or some-other-fucking-where, and in an interview said, 'Thank God I got there first and these people heard my music. I mean, can you imagine if Ozzy Osbourne had got there first and they had to deal with his music?'

I was like, Who the fuck do you think you are to say that? Who says your music is better? Who is it for you to belittle this genre of music?

Then, at the end of the last episode of the first season of *The Osbournes* in May 2002, they did a question-and-answer round-up of Ozzy's life. The last question to Ozzy was: 'Ozzy, sum your life up.' And he looked at the camera and said, 'I'm not proud of everything I've done. I'm not proud of having a poor education. I'm not proud of being dyslexic. I'm not proud of being an alcoholic drug addict. I'm not proud of biting the head off a bat. I'm not proud of having attention-deficit disorder. But I'm a real guy. To be Ozzy Osbourne . . . it could be worse. I could be Sting.'

When the show was sold to Channel 4, they took huge bill-boards all over the country. It was basically a picture of us with that quote from Ozzy: 'It could be worse. I could be Sting.'

So these ads went up everywhere, all over the under-ground, on thirty-foot hoardings across the country, and Sting was devastated. Not that he said anything to us but we heard from mutual friends that he was very upset, and that his children were very upset. So from then on it was open season. Them against us. Thanks to the success of *The Osbournes*, the balance had totally shifted. From my perspective it was like,

You've been running my husband down since the eighties, so cool it, back off, because we can fucking retaliate.

So, anyway, a few years ago, we turn up at the Grammy's in LA, and we're all there, Ozzy, me and the kids going down the red carpet, and just in front of us is Sting with Trudie. Suddenly he stops in mid-carpet, and turns around to Ozzy.

'Let's call it a truce,' he said.

And Trudie said to me, 'Let's stop this, because of the children.'

And I said, 'You are absolutely right, I want it to end.' And we all hugged and it ended.

At that point Sting went up in my estimation. He was man enough to do that. I honestly think it had reached the point where it was getting to his children. I know how things like that affect mine, so I related to that.

I still think he's a musical snob, but he's by no means the only one. During the eighties and nineties there was great snobbery in popular music, and people would constantly be putting down heavy metal and hard-edge music. But now that genre is part of the rock and roll heritage, and it's accepted and respected as such. When Ozzy got inducted into the Rock and Roll Hall of Fame in March 2006 at the Waldorf-Astoria in New York, Sting was there and he went up and congratulated him.

'It's been a long time coming, and you really deserve it,' Sting said. And he hugged him.

What changed his mind, I think, was when Ozzy found his voice and answered back. He had to take notice.

Sting was big enough to call off a feud that had been running for years, and I respect him for that. And it meant I could sit happily with him and Trudie that night at the Roundhouse – we had a great evening, and the auction raised a million pounds for the Trust. As for my speech – it went down like a nun's knickers.

Only a few days after the Prince's Trust event, I found myself caught up in another slanging match very much against my will, and again it was because someone attacked my husband. But this time things didn't end so well.

As tension builds on *The X-Factor* leading up to the final, it's become tradition that we get a few celebrities along to the show. It's a fun night for them, and sometimes they get to be involved, if not on camera, then during the commercial break. The audience enjoys it, everyone enjoys it.

So it's 18 November 2006 and things are hotting up. During a commercial break, one of the warm-up guys asks the audience if they have any questions for the panel. Another tradition. It's not recorded, just an opportunity for us all to relax and have a laugh. On this particular night, Chris Tarrant is in the audience. I'd spotted him already, sitting on the other side of the aisle to Ricky Gervais. He says he has a question and the warm-up guy passes him the mike.

'Louis,' he begins. So Louis stands up. This is also the tradition. 'We all know that you're the best judge, that you're the one that's got their finger on the pulse of the music industry. We've got you to thank for all these brilliant bands. We know that you're the guy really.' Applause. Louis smiles, takes a little bow and sits down. OK. Not a question, but OK.

'Sharon.' I stand up. 'You are beautiful, warm and caring – and you are married to the most articulate man in the world. And the best-dressed.'

The sarcastic words, the grin, the red face – everything collides and it's like a nuclear explosion inside me. 'Don't you DARE talk about my fucking family, you shut your mouth, you cunt.' I could feel myself shaking and blood was pounding in my ears. The grin on his face had disappeared and the whole place was silent, just the 't' of 'cunt' bouncing off the studio walls.

'Listen, you,' I say, finger jabbing, 'don't you try to get a cheap laugh on my husband. He's one of the most loved men in this country. Don't you try to get a cheap laugh on his back. He's not even here. If you want to get a laugh, talk about you. What about you, you lying piece of shit? At least my husband and I are a team.'

'Well, what about you getting fired off another show—'

'I couldn't give a fuck. You piece of shit. Go fuck yourself. Get out of this studio.'

So then he tries to redeem himself to the audience. Says how he's known Ozzy for twenty-five years and they are really good friends.

'You lying sonofabitch.' I fume. 'You don't know my

husband. You fucking ignored my husband because you didn't think he was good enough to be sat at a table with you.'

It was only at this point that I remembered where I was and who was there. I caught sight of the silent faces of children in the audience and I thought: Oh Shit.

It was wrong of me. So wrong. Later some people asked if there was any baggage between Chris Tarrant and me. It depends what you mean. What I said was true. On the one occasion we had sat at the same table, he had ignored us. If that's baggage, then yes, we had baggage. It was the Pride of Britain Awards and we were sitting with the Prime Minister as he then was, Tony Blair, and his wife. Piers Morgan was at the same table – he was editor of the *Mirror* at the time. It was early in 2004 and Ozzy was still recovering from the accident that nearly killed him, and this was one of his first public outings. Everybody else thought we were fit to talk to, asking Ozzy how he was and the rest of it, but Chris Tarrant never so much as acknowledged either of us, never even gave us eye contact. Fine. Then we saw him again, at something like the Brit Awards, some TV award show, and again, he totally blanked us. So we don't know him and he doesn't know us.

There are times, when you work in the same industry, when you may not know somebody, in the sense that you haven't worked together or been formally introduced, but you go, 'Hi, how are you?' But with him and a few other people, you get this kind of invisible force field around them that says,

'No further. Don't talk to me. Not interested.' So you respect that. You may not like it, but OK. Don't want to talk to you anyway. Got no common ground. See ya. Next. No big deal.

I have never had a conversation with this man in my life. Never shook his hand. Never mentioned that I think he looks like a garden gnome. Nothing. However, I used words that were totally inappropriate.

But I wouldn't go to his show on a Saturday night and make a sarcastic remark about one of his family. Why would I? What would I possibly get from that? This may not be my show, but I'm employed to work on it. And I've been at this studio for three years, and basically you're on my turf.

He can say what he likes about me with that sarcastic, studenty wit of his. He can say that I look like a drag queen, or that I am the luckiest woman in the industry to have a job. There are any number of digs he can take at me. But my husband isn't even here to defend himself. Why would you try and get a cheap laugh on somebody that isn't even in the room?

So what is so superior about him that he can make judgements on other people? All I know about Chris Tarrant, with his awful white hair and his beer-drinker's face and beer-drinker's belly, is that he did *TISWAS* – a kid's show that involved such interesting things as throwing custard over people – and now he does *Who Wants To Be A Millionaire?*, and that for years he lived a lie with his family. Because all this happened around the time his affair was being exposed in the press. So how clever do you have to be, when your trousers are down around your ankles, to attack someone who's famous for saying, 'You start on my family and I'll bite your arse.'

During the next commercial break, we all leave the stage and Simon Cowell comes up to me looking like fury.

'Apologise to him.'

I'm like, 'Apologise for what, Simon?'

'What you did was totally inappropriate. Apologise to the man.'

'For what? For defending myself and my family? I will not apologise to him. He should apologise to me. I was in my place of work, I was doing nothing wrong and he's trying to get a cheap laugh on the back of my husband. He was asked if he had a question for one of the judges. It wasn't recital time. This wasn't a forum for Chris Tarrant to get laughs. He stands up, not with a question but with a monologue. So my point is, Simon, I did nothing wrong. I did nothing wrong. Who the fuck is he that I should apologise?'

Simon turns his back to me and walks away. Then a producer appears.

'Sharon. You have to go out there and apologise for your language.'

I said, 'You're right. I have to. To the audience.'

And I did. I went into the studio and apologised. We didn't have long because we didn't have much time before the cameras began to roll again.

'It's a family show,' I said, 'and I forgot that, so I'm sorry for using foul language, and I apologise for that. But I'm not sorry for what I said to him.'

That night on my way home I realised that, yet again, Simon was right. He's always called me the loose cannon. And I am.

Of course, it got into the press, even though it was all off-camera. Several days later our publicist Gary Farrow put out a statement saying something like, 'It's all over now. Gone and forgotten.' Chris Tarrant, the wanker, texted Gary and said, 'Don't you ever speak for me, it's not gone and it's not forgotten.'

We had another month on the show and Simon continued to be upset right up till the end of the series. My point was that Chris Tarrant didn't work for him; they don't have a friendship. So what did it matter to him? That it might reflect badly on the programme? I don't think so.

Loyalty is incredibly important in my life: loyalty to my family, loyalty to people I work with, who for me are like an extended family. If anyone had done that to Simon, I would have stood up for him. I'd always have his back. I am not upset that Simon didn't come to my defence; I understand. He's a professional and I should never have used the words I did. But anyway, just for luck, one more time: Chris Tarrant is a cunt. As Ozzy says, 'My wife is a pit bull. She'll jump out of the window and rip your head off if you say the wrong thing to me or the kids.'

Why are people so shocked when I come across as confrontational, when they see me being considerate and respectful in other circumstances? They seem to think that one of these sides of my personality must be an act. Why do they think you have to be one thing or the other? Why can't a person be sensitive but strong at the same time? And if this means being confrontational sometimes, then what's wrong with that? Can't you be a sympathetic person when somebody is asking you for advice, but also be honest and sharp-tongued when somebody close to you is attacked? I don't go looking for confrontation, but I'm old enough now to have earned the right to speak my mind when I need to.

It's an odd thing that when you're famous, people think they have the right to say whatever they like about you. Things they would never dream of saying to a stranger, or even someone they know, they'll happily say right to your face, just because you're on TV. It's like they think you're not real – that you don't have real feelings. In summer 2005 I was on my way to a business appointment when a Channel 4 camera crew stopped me in the street. There was a film screening going on nearby and they thought I was attending, but in fact I just happened to be there at the same time. It turned out they were part of a spoof 'comedy' team. What I didn't know was that the microphone was hiding a water pistol. After shoving the mike in my face and asking me some questions, they then squirted water all over me. They did the same thing to Tom Cruise a couple of weeks later at the *War of the Worlds* premiere. That time they were arrested, but I didn't wait for the police. I ran into a nearby restaurant, got the waiters to fill up a champagne bucket with ice, ran back out and tipped it over them. All over the camera, everything.

It didn't bother me – it was just a stupid prank. But it's a good example of how people think that if you're famous then you're always fair game. But I wasn't there for the screening – I was just going about my business. They would never squirt water over a regular member of the public like that. It's like they think we're cartoon characters or something – not real.

Two years later another complete stranger attacked me for no apparent reason. But this time they made the mistake of bringing my family into it.

When ABC had first approached me to do *Dancing with the Stars*, they had one condition. 'You have to have your red hair,' they said. It wasn't a deal breaker, but it was like, 'Come on. Go red.' It was how America thought of me. My trademark. So time to see Kay, who I'd been going to for years at her salon in the Beverly Hills Hotel.

My hair is my Achilles heel. It's been completely white since my late twenties, so by the time the cancer happened I'd been dyeing it for twenty years. I should have left it then, let it grow back to its natural colour, but I couldn't do that to the family. It would have been too much of a shock. First I had wigs made and then it was back to dyeing it the colour that had become my trademark since *The Osbournes*, the spiky red.

Red on white is very high maintenance. Every ten days the roots get done brown, then every few weeks the red spikes gets added.

Then – just before the second series of *The X-Factor* – it just gave up, broke off half an inch from my scalp. I looked like a dog with mange, and we had to do something. I mean, I was going to be on television! Ozzy's nephew, always known as Cousin Terry, is a hairdresser specialising in extensions, so the moment I arrived in England he came and sorted me out. In an attempt to lessen the amount of colour that was going on my hair, I decided to go blonde. Hardly anybody liked it. Simon Cowell hated it, Ozzy hated it. Now ABC were saying they hated it. So, OK.

So one afternoon I'm sitting there at Kay's salon down in the basement of the Beverly Hills Hotel getting everything done. Dyed, spiked, cut, a manicure, a pedicure, the lot. I had Melinda come with her laptop, together with Michael who runs my office in LA, so as we could do some work, because otherwise I'd just be gossiping with Kay. So I'm sitting there with my feet in a bowl of hot water and my head in tin foil, Melinda one side of me and Michael the other, when this woman comes in. Turns out she's got an appointment with Kay but she's early. Apparently she'd been in a couple of times before but didn't live in LA.

Anyway, she's giving me the evil eye, but I pay no any attention. So Kay says to this woman, 'You're half an hour early. D'you wanna take a cup of coffee and come back?' So she does, goes away and then comes back, but Kay still hasn't finished with me. So she puts the lady in the chair, then she's taking out the foil from my hair and this woman continues to stare at me. I take no notice and carry on going through things with Michael and Melinda. As for the woman, I honestly thought she was not well. She was the kind of person that you look away from when they give you eye contact.

So while I'm being washed, Kay's talking to this woman about her hair and what she wants done to it – the salon is tiny, so multi-client conversations are standard practice – and without any real warning the woman blurts out:

'Who does she think she is? I pay like she does and you've gotta spend the time on my hair.'

All other voices stopped – there were another couple of people in the salon – all you could hear was the whirr of a hairdryer.

'What did you say?' I said.

'I said, who do you think you are? I pay like you do. Who do you think you are?'

'Look here, missus. I don't even know you. Why are you starting a problem? I've been coming here for twenty years. Just relax. You'll get your hair done. What's your problem?'

'I know about you. I know who you are. I know all about you.'

'Well, I know fuck all about you except you need a fuck-ing bra and a bit of make-up,' I said. Which was true, which is probably why she didn't take it too well. She had the kind of pendulous breasts where the nipples are facing south. Out of the corner of my eye, I could see Melinda's shoulders shaking and Michael's eyes were rolling.

'How *dare* you talk to me like this,' she huffed. 'How dare you.' By this time her nostrils were flaring. Like I said, it's a small place and you can see that sort of thing.

'Oh fuck off!'

'*And* I know about your children.'

Well, that did it. I got up from the chair, my hair dripping from a back wash, and in one step I had my finger an inch from her nose.

'You shut your fucking mouth. Now. D'you hear?' I snarled. I wanted to get her miserable face and squeeze it with my hands.

'I know about your children. I've read about them.'

'Don't you ever mention my children. You know nothing about my children. You get out of my face before I fucking take your face off your head.'

'I'm going to sue you!'

'Good.'

'I'm going to get the police!'

'Get 'em. Just get the fuck out of here!'

At this point Kay intervened.

'You no talk about children,' she said to the woman. 'You go now. You go now.'

At this, the woman swivels her chair and directs her venom at Kay.

Father and daughter. Twenty years separate these two pictures.

Ozzy as seen by Andy Warhol. The woman with the hair is Dianne Brill, a New York socialite, known as the feminist femme fatale, who was part of Warhol's circus. We weren't.

At the MTV video awards in Australia in 2005: Anna Nicole Smith, me, Carmen Electra and Kelly. I really took to Anna Nicole Smith and was very sad when I heard that she had died. Such a tragedy in someone so young and beautiful.
(© ALPHA Press Agency)

Playing celebrities at Fashion Rocks in Monaco: Kelly, Donatella Versace, Mariah Carey, Ozzy and me.
(© Jason Fraser)

'Drama drops' – with my partner in laughter and crime, Lisa Riley.

*The Vagina Monologues*. How many ways are there to fake an orgasm on stage?

First night team photo in Newcastle: Jenny Jules, Lisa Riley, stage manager Lizzie Chapman, Jude, me and Kel.

Fearne Cotton and me presenting *Top of the Pops* in 2006. Who knew we would end up working together on *The X-Factor*?

(© ALPHA Press Agency)

Ozzy performing at the thirtieth anniversary concert for the Prince's Trust at the Tower of London in May 2006. (© ITV plc/Clarence House)

Kelly, Ozzy and me with Prince Charles at the line-up after the show at the Tower. It was the second time in two months we had been at an event with the Prince. The previous occasion was a private dinner at Windsor Castle. (© ITV plc/Clarence House)

Ozzy and Marilyn.

Our agent Rob Light claimed that Iron Maiden's singer was as famous as Ozzy. I told him that people on the street wouldn't have a clue who Bruce Dickinson was. He took up my challenge with these posters, and had the grace to admit he was wrong.

Jack at Ozzfest, 2006. Jack has his own life now, but he still loves getting involved when he can.

Ozzfest 2006. San Bernardino is the big LA date. Here I am in true managerial mode.

'As for you,' she says, with a look-at-me-I'm-a-person-too attitude, 'I tipped you ten dollars the last time I was here. You can't treat me like this.' And then she leaves. Flounces out. We all breathe a sigh of relief. Michael tries to look stern but can't hold it, and he's soon giggling with the rest of us.

'Fuck off and get the police,' I shout at the footsteps retreating down the corridor. 'What the fuck do I care!'

Five minutes later the husband's on the phone. 'We're suing you,' he says to Kay. And that's not all. Turns out she still wants her hair done. So poor Kay had to do this woman's hair three times in the next week to make up for the 'unpleasantness', and not charge her one single dollar.

Slanging matches of any kind are best avoided, particularly when they involve the press, but sometimes there's no other way of dealing with the situation. You would think by now that people would know not to attack my family. I wonder sometimes if they do it just to get publicity. In my eyes that's the worst. It's so pathetic, criticising other people's success just to get your own name in the paper. In May 2007 a certain ageing rocker made that mistake.

Ozzy was about to embark on his first solo European tour since his accident in 2004. We landed in London on 24 May. The following day Ozzy was booked to do *Jonathan Ross* to promote his gigs at Wembley and Birmingham later in June. Just as we're about to set off for the studio I get a call from LA. All hell had let loose.

One of the people copying *The Osbournes* format was a

rock and roller called Gene Simmons. He is the front man from Kiss – a band that's better known for its make-up than its music. Around our house he's famous for being a tedious show-off. We've known him for years – Kiss had their first big tour supporting Sabbath in 1975. He's a very weird character in my view – he reminds me of Fagin. It's all 'have I got a deal for you'. His only conversation is sex and money. If he's not showing Ozzy his Kiss watch, he's showing him his Kiss shoes, his Kiss credit card. And worse. 'Hey, Ozzy, guess what, you can get buried in a Kiss coffin.' I mean – who would brag about that?

To my face he's 'Oh Sharon, you're so great, what a great business move that was.' But when he talks to you, his eyes are darting all around to see what else is going on. You never really get his full attention. He came up with a great concept for Kiss, but as a human being my experience with him has always been pretty distasteful. I find him offensive. Everything he talks about has a sexual connotation. You see him around with all these sad-looking eighties-style groupies, and it's 'Have you met my sister' and other corny one-liners. Everything has to be about him. 'I'm doing this show, I'm doing that show, I'm earning thousands of dollars' . . . and who gives a shit.

The Gene Simmons reality show is called *Family Jewels* and he's doing it with his partner and their two children. The programme is about as copycat as you can get: the rock and roller, the house, the dogs, the kids. The only difference is that he's not married to his partner and he's always talking about women and licking and other shit in the same nauseating, lascivious vein. His pièce de résistance is claiming to have slept with 14,897 women, or something equally ridiculous.

Because a lot of journalists are basically lazy, *Family Jewels* is often compared to *The Osbournes*. However, whenever someone doing a magazine or TV interview dares to suggest that his show might be a rip-off of ours, he disagrees. 'We're nothing like *The Osbournes*,' he says. Now that's standard. Then some time in May, *Blender* magazine ran another of these banal interviews, with the same banal answer, except that this time he expanded it. 'There's no comparison between us and the Osbournes,' he whined, adding, 'My children aren't addicts. My children are great.'

Immediately phones start ringing, emails buzzing backwards and forwards, and *Blender* asks me for a comment.

A comment? Sure, I'd give them a comment.

'The trouble with Gene Simmons,' I said, 'is that he will always be a C-list celebrity and his wife's snatch has been rubbed on every brass pole in LA. I'll fucking tear his head off and stick it up his wife's cunt!'

It wasn't entirely accurate. I don't know why I said 'wife' because part of the storyline (if you can call it that) of his show is that the parents have an open relationship. His non-wife, Shannon Tweed, used to be a centrefold in the Hugh Hefner era. Personally I don't think it can be nice for the woman to be constantly told that the person who fathered her kids refuses to marry her. When anyone says, 'Oh, we want an open marriage – it works for us that way', I'm not convinced. I think it's all fluff. It might work for the man, but for the non-wife it's humiliating. Gene Simmons's whole thing is 'I've bedded three million women and my tongue is longer than a fucking snake's.' It's all bullshit. But I don't think it's nice for any woman to suffer that.

So anyway, I gave it to him and to her. (On reflection, I regret bringing Shannon into it, because she didn't say anything negative in the interview.) There were no reper-cussions. As a father himself Gene should have known better than to start on my kids. He's nearly sixty, for fuck's sake. He can say whatever he wants about me. I can defend myself if the fucker wants to have a go. That's an absolutely open play-ing field. But he didn't learn the cardinal rule when dealing with Mrs O: you hurt me and I will hurt you. You hurt my family and I will hurt you. And what he said was just cruel and unnecessary and untrue. I would never attack his chil-dren. I don't know them but I have to say that they look like decent kids. And who am I to make a comment about any-body's children? If a journalist says, 'Don't you think you're like the Osbournes?' by all means say, 'No, we've got noth-ing in common.' But don't say, 'Because *my* kids aren't addicts.' For the record, Gene Simmons is a pathetic has-been with one of the worst wigs I have ever seen in my life. And just one more thing, Mr Simmons. You might have a huge ego and a huge tongue but I daresay a very important part of your body isn't as big.


I try my best not to get pulled into fights these days, but I will always defend myself if I'm attacked and I'm not afraid to say what I think. I have to be frank and honest. I think it's because when I was younger I got into so much trouble trying to please people, trying to be accepted, trying to tell people what they wanted to hear. But when I was doing it, it felt wrong, and I could feel my stomach twisting as if it was full of knots. I don't want to be like that any more. Obviously I try to be polite, but I'm not going to bullshit. Ozzy always says that you need to have a really good memory if you're going to bullshit, just to remember what you said to this person, to that person. When you lie it's all so much trouble. It's so much easier just to tell the truth.

Sometimes I wish I did have a filter on my mouth, though. In March this year Prince Charles invited Ozzy and me to a special, private event at Windsor Castle. Welders, our house in Buckinghamshire, is only about twenty minutes away by car, and over the years we've been countless times to the castle itself, but this was the first time we'd been there without having to pay the entrance fee.

The occasion was a dinner given as part of the thirty years' celebrations for the Prince's Trust. In every possible way it was a night to remember. I wore a beautiful Vivienne Westwood gown – it was navy and black with a train and a bit of a plunge, and very caught in at the waist. By the time we got there, the sky was dark and the castle all lit up – it really did feel like a fairytale. Instead of tourists and guides and children running around, like we were used to, there were footmen with trays of canapés and glasses of champagne, and people in fabulous dresses, and jewels twinkling on ears and bosoms.

If all this wasn't enough, when it came to dinner I found I was sitting next to the Prince. We talked about architecture and art. We talked about drugs and I told him about Jack, how he overcame his addiction and that now he lectures at schools in America. He's tried to do the same in England, but the Department of Education won't allow it. The Prince was genuinely amazed. I explained that it's because the government doesn't recognise alcoholism as an illness. He said he'd like to talk to Jack about it – 'and I'll see what I can do'. It hasn't happened yet, but it will, I know.

Anyway, a woman sitting nearby looked like she was being unbelievably boring. Everyone round her looked bored.

'Don't you ever get tired of talking to these people?' I asked him, as we both glanced over at her.

'Not in that way,' he said. 'Because everybody here has made a difference with my charity.' But he confessed that he did get incredibly tired.

That man's schedule is unbelievable. He can go to three different cities in a day, every day. And everywhere he goes he has to make polite, superficial chat. He has to know who these people are, be prepped before every meeting. OK, so it comes with the territory, but it's gruelling.

The boring woman had an unfortunate patch of soreness on both sides of her mouth that made her look a bit like the Joker. I turned my head towards the Prince's ear.

'You know what's the matter with her, don't you, sir?'

'No.'

'She sucks too much dick.'

His eyes rolled into the back of his head. He died.

Kelly has definitely inherited her mother's frankness, and one particular comment has gone down in family history. It happened one Christmas a few years ago.

Before he became famous as a celebrity jeweller, Theo Fennell started off as a silversmith, and I have bought loads of stuff from him over the years. Not only the usual bracelets, rings and necklaces, but silver containers for traditional condiments, like Heinz Ketchup and Marmite and Tabasco, so that if you put one of these kitchen bottles on the dining-room table it still looks elegant. I started buying from him about twenty years ago, because he was making crosses long before crosses were fashionable. In those days he only had a little shop on the Fulham Road, in Chelsea. Now he is a huge success with shops-within-shops in Harvey Nichols and Selfridges, and the original shop in the Fulham Road has expanded, though it is still quite small.

Anyway, every year he hosts an unmissable Christmas party. Only about thirty or so people are invited, and it's always amazing. Amazing food, amazing entertainment. Because it is so intimate, you feel extremely privileged to have been invited. Usually we all try to go, but Jack was working on his television series so it was just Ozzy, Aimee, Kelly and me, and that year Louis came too.

The whole shop is taken over by the party and, as the space is small, you are always very close to the entertainer, who on this occasion was a stripper magician, and she was doing extraordinary things like putting out cigarettes in her fanny, not to mention extracting streams of red handkerchiefs from the same place, though not at the same time. So Elton was there and David and their friend Patrick Cox, and Lulu was there and Hugh Grant with Jemima Khan, and, of course, Theo and his wife and daughter. Theo is very English and a very handsome man, inside and out – a huge personality. His wife and daughter are equally lovely. So the whole thing is beautifully done and we sit down at the various tables to have dinner.

Kelly found herself sitting next to Hugh Grant. His girl-friend Jemima Khan was the other side. From where I sat I had a good look at her and was not impressed. She was very sour-faced and spent the entire dinner twiddling her hair, making little corkscrews with her finger, like a sulky fourteen-year-old. She never introduced herself, never said good evening and made us feel we weren't welcome at her table, directing all her attention to the person at the other side of her – I can't remember who that was.

So Hugh Grant turns to Kelly, and she goes, 'Hi, I'm Kelly.' And he goes, 'Hi, I'm Hugh.' There's a pause. Then his eyebrows go up and he tilts his head to one side in that innocent little-boy way.

'They tell me,' he said, 'that you're on television. I don't watch television, so perhaps you could tell me what do you do?'

'Not a lot,' Kelly replied. 'But then I don't know much about you either, other than you fuck prostitutes.'

He was stunned. Speechless. We have all seen that Hugh Grant stunned-and-speechless look up on the screen, and now there it was, a couple of feet away, in the flesh and for real.

But my mouthy daughter hadn't finished. 'And, by the way,' she added, 'that prostitute was better-looking than the girlfriend you're with tonight.'

Well, that kinda set the tone at our table. Actually it was funny. I laughed. Couldn't help it. Hugh Grant's face had been enough. I wasn't upset by Kelly's remarks because I don't think anybody else heard but him and me, and I thought that his girlfriend was rude anyway. Like an iceberg. That's how she seemed to me. I have seen her on several occasions since, and she is still an iceberg. Which is fine. I don't know her. She doesn't know me. But from one woman to another, you usually nod heads when you pass at an event. An acknowledgement that says, 'Yes, I have seen you before.'

Hugh Grant, on the other hand, has a great sense of

humour. We have seen him any number of times since that Christmas party, and we always have a laugh. Every time we see him we say, 'Oh, just so's you know, you're sitting next to Kelly tonight,' and he runs! Kelly was very young and very ballsy at the time, and although we've never talked about it, I think he got it.

# Hollywood

I give a chuckle now, remembering what Kelly said. Poor old Hugh Grant. Don would have loved that story – he never took shit from anybody.

When my father fell ill, I realised I had to reconcile with him. So I sat the kids down and told them the whole story. And I explained to them that now they had to make a choice, whether they wanted their grandfather in their lives or not. It was up to them, and of course I would understand either way.

Kelly and Jack decided to meet him. They were curious and wanted to know about their grandfather. So they met him, but he wasn't the man he once was. The Don Arden I'd known no longer existed. By now he was already sick, a little old man with scared eyes.

But Aimee said something interesting. She thought about it for a while and then she said, 'Mum, I've decided. I don't want to meet him.' And I was like, Well that's fine, Aimee, that's your decision and I respect that. But when I asked why, she said, 'I don't want to learn to love him only for him to die.' And I understood. Completely. He was already so sick. She kept to her decision. She only saw Don twice – once when Ozzy and I reaffirmed our vows, but by then he didn't recognise any of us. And then again, just a few weeks ago. And she did that for me, not for her – my smart, sensitive little girl.

When I was growing up, I could never call anything my own. One minute you had a piece of jewellery, a fur coat, a watch. The next it was down the pawnshop. Even as I got older, nothing was safe. The houses, the cars. Don would say they were yours, and the next it was – I need them back. Nothing was permanent.

But when I first held Aimee in my arms – so beautiful, so vulnerable – I realised, she's mine. No one can ever take her away from me. Not the bailiffs, not a thief, not my father, nobody. And it was then I knew that everything else was just bullshit. The crazy life I was leading, my father's hold over me, all the family feuds – it was just complete bullshit. And nothing was ever the same again. Falling in love with Ozzy changed me, but it was having Aimee, and then Kelly and Jack, that made me realise I could choose a different life. My amazing family.

It's funny how things have turned out. There was my father always saying how important his family was to him. Forever going on about, 'Oh, this is for my wife, for my family, I'm such a loyal husband, it's all for them'. And all the time he had a mistress, another life. It felt like such a betrayal at the time. I had believed in this whole fictional character he had created for himself, and when I found out it wasn't real, I felt like such an idiot to have believed in him.

Now, of course, I know that he did love us all very much. Passionately. But the way he presented himself to the world and the way he was really – they were two separate things. Like he was an actor. Playing a role.

By the time my father came back into our lives, *The Osbournes* was a huge hit around the world. One of the reasons I think the show was such a success was because people saw that no matter what was going on – all the drama and the fighting – the bottom line was, we all loved each other so much. We are such a loving family, even when we're screaming at each other.

But what I hadn't counted on was just how famous it would make us. I could never have guessed just what a phenomenon the show would be – who could? We were celebrities overnight. The only person whose life it didn't change was Ozzy. He already had huge fame and credibility as a musician and as a songwriter. But for the rest of us, suddenly the spotlight was on us. Life would never be the same again. Like it or not, we were now celebrities, and caught up in that whole crazy world.

# 4

## Celebrity

Kelly called me from England very early one morning, ecstatic. She'd seen a couple of photos of her dad that she wanted to buy.

'Why would I ever want to buy a photograph of your dad, Kelly?'

'Because, Mum, they're by Andy Warhol.'

And then I remembered.

It was the late eighties, less than a year before Warhol died. We had just flown into New York and Ozzy was in a very strange mood. I remember being in the back of a limousine driving from JFK across the Brooklyn Bridge into Manhattan, when Susan Blond, a publicist for Sony, called to say Andy Warhol wanted to meet Ozzy.

She later claimed to be Warhol's muse – she was certainly part of the Warhol circus. Obviously Ozzy and I were intrigued to meet him, so we said, Let's do it.

First came dinner. They had taken over a room in a restaurant down in Greenwich Village somewhere, and his whole entourage was there, plus Susan Blond and her partner, and Ozzy and myself. There were probably about sixteen people in all – Warhol always went round in a group – a real motley crew. There was this woman who looked like a drag queen and a couple of huge gay guys.

Ozzy and I were given chairs opposite Warhol. He was in his late fifties, about fifty-eight, though the strangest fifty-eight-year-old you could imagine – exactly like you see him in pictures but more exaggerated. Skinny face, and he didn't have a lot of flesh on him – his collar was too big for his neck, so the effect was a bit tortoise-like. He sat right across the table from us, looking gaunt and pale with these big black glasses on. Most of the time he didn't say anything, and when he did, it was so quiet you couldn't really hear. He had this little camera on the table by him, and every so often he'd take a photograph. It was some kind of instamatic camera – very basic with no lenses or anything like that. Throughout most of the dinner he was whispering in his partner's ear. He was like a voyeur.

Dinner over, he said he wanted to take us all to a club. So off we went. I have no idea now where it was – downtown Manhattan somewhere – all I remember is the noise. Even though we were in a roped-off VIP area, you couldn't hear a word anyone was saying. It wasn't long before Ozzy was getting agitated. It just wasn't his scene at all, and he didn't have any patience for it.

'I'm bored,' he told me. And I'm like, 'So am I, but we can't leave yet, it would be rude. Just give it another half an hour, and then we can disappear.' I was sitting there like a great big Yorkshire pudding, hideously out of place in my Laura Ashley-style smock dress. Everybody in Warhol's entourage looked like they'd just fallen out of a fashion shoot for *Vogue*. They all looked like Isabella Blow. The men looked like male models. And I looked like a Yorkshire pudding.

Ozzy said he was going to the bathroom. Meanwhile, I'm sipping on my Coca-Cola, nobody addressing any conversation to me, just staring. I'm sure they were thinking, Who the fuck is she?, and I was thinking, Who the fuck are they?

I get to the end of my Coca-Cola and my husband still hasn't returned. I begin to panic. I go to the bathroom. He's not there. I start running frantically round the club in my lovely black comfortable shoes (with, of course, a matching handbag).

And then it clicks. The bastard had left me. The fucker. I was planning my attack on him while at the same time trying to get myself a taxi out of there. What was I to do? My husband had gone with the car. I'm in a club somewhere in New York – I have no idea where I am. I was too embarrassed to go back into the roped-off area and say I was leaving, and that

Ozzy had gone. I just wanted to do a runner. So that's exactly what I did. A taxi back to the hotel.

Ozzy arrived back at around six in the morning. He told me he'd bonded with the limousine driver, who knew where to get some good coke. And that was much more appealing for Ozzy than to sit in a club with Andy Warhol.

At one point in the evening Warhol had taken some pictures of Ozzy with the big blonde woman who looked like a drag queen – totally over the top, one of the travelling circus. Her name was Dianne Brill and she was known as the feminist femme fatale. Jerry Hall is quoted as saying that if you went to a party and Dianne Brill was there, you were at the right party. Not if you were me, you weren't. I wasn't a happening person. I looked like I was someone's mother who'd just come in from the Bronx. You look at a picture and you think, What is wrong with this picture? What the fuck is that woman doing there?

Now I'd say, 'I'm uncomfortable, I'm leaving.' Ozzy had the right idea at the time.

So, nearly twenty years on Kelly had found the photographs Warhol had taken that evening. They were owned by the Warhol Foundation in Pittsburgh. We decided we had to get them. Although I didn't like his scene, I had always admired Warhol as an artist, as did Kelly. When she started earning money, she began to collect his work – which is what she was doing at the gallery in the first place.

Of course, Andy Warhol is known for saying that 'in the

future everybody will be famous for fifteen minutes'. Looking at the explosion of reality TV shows and celebrity magazines, I think he has probably been proved right.

I remember when Jack heard that line, he said, 'Well, I'm just glad my fifteen minutes are over', and I know what he means. It's one thing to be doing something you love, which happens to make you famous in the process. Like Ozzy: for him, the music always comes first. And I love the work I do – judging new talent. It's like an extension of what I've always done as a rock manager. Jack's TV show *Adrenaline Junkie* is all about doing the things he's passionate about, though I have to say, as a mother, some of the things he does worry the shit out of me.

But there are some people who chase fame just for fame's sake. They're desperate for it. Either that or they see your fame and they're jealous of it. They want a piece of it, of what you've achieved. Fame can make people very ugly.

For every successful movie or songwriter, there's an insect crawling out of the woodwork saying, 'That was my idea, you stole it.' And I still can't get my head round someone saying that about *The Osbournes*. But that's America, in particular. Once you have a hit show, once you're famous, you might as well sit by the letterbox and wait for the lawsuits to come through the door. Some people have said to me that, in a way, getting a lawsuit in LA is the real sign that you've made it. If that's true then we really fucking made it – because we had not one but two lawsuits against *The Osbournes*, and it was only after four terrible years that the nightmare finally came to an end.

Although nobody won, we definitely lost. Eventually, everything was settled out of court simply because we were haemorrhaging so much money on lawyers we had to apply a tourniquet to avoid bleeding to death. It costs us nine million dollars in legal fees alone.

*The Osbournes* first hit the airwaves in March 2002, although we'd had the cameras in the house since the previous autumn. The first episode had us moving into the house in Doheny, the children back at school, everyone getting on with their lives.

The idea sprang from a documentary done by an English production company called September Films. *Ozzy Osbourne Uncut* had gone on to win the Rose D'Or at the Montreux International Television Festival in Switzerland. I decided the idea had more mileage than just a European one-off, and contacted MTV to see if they'd be interested in doing something along the same lines. They agreed to commission three episodes.

To say that *The Osbournes* was a hit is the understatement of the century. I always knew that Ozzy was a comic genius but the success of the show took everybody totally by surprise. Unfortunately, life has a habit of knocking you back just when you think you're safe, and less than three months after that first broadcast, I was diagnosed with colon cancer. Then, in July 2002 – my original operation having been successful – I had a relapse and was rushed back into Cedars-Sinai. So there I was: semi-conscious, mid-blood transfusion, when a man finds his way into my room and prods me with an envelope. At least that's what they told me later. I have no memory of it. It turned out he was serving me with a writ. In American law all you have to do is touch the person and that's enough. Needless to say the doctors went insane, but that's another story.

That was the first of two lawsuits by two separate sets of people. The general thrust of both of them was that *The Osbournes* was their idea. That it was scripted. It was never scripted. Can you imagine anyone scripting Ozzy? Can you imagine anyone scripting my cancer? A great storyline, that. It was a reality show.

Four years of torture followed. Four years of sleepless nights and misery. These vultures were claiming not only Ozzy's and my money, but the kids' money too.

The truth is that once you get sued in America you are basically fucked. Well, I'm a fighter and I was not prepared to pay these bloodsuckers to go away. Perhaps I should have done. But when you're entirely innocent it goes against the grain to say you're guilty, even if everybody is telling you it's easier that way.

When I sold the idea to MTV, the phrase 'reality show' had been used for fly-on-the-wall documentaries, but never for anything involving a celebrity. Yet from the minute *The Osbournes* aired, the face of TV changed, for good and for bad and probably for ever – and our lives changed with it. In less than a beat it was an epidemic. First came other musicians, other rock and rollers that thought: Hey, I'm crazy, I've got a wife and kids! Why not me? Gradually it trickled down through the music hierarchy to record producers. Hey, my life's interesting! My family's different! Then came the models, the half-arsed actors, gangsters, bounty hunters, even a family that ran a mortuary.

So far there have been about sixty 'reality family' series across America, and I'm not even counting the ones that never made it past the pilot stage. Of these, perhaps three have been successful. Eventually it will dry up; crazy soon wears thin.

That was why we quit when we did. It was the beginning of our third season. Crazy families were over the networks like a rash. I knew then it had to be the last. There wasn't one net-work in America that wasn't trying to jump on the conveyor belt, trying to find their own *Osbournes*. But of course they couldn't. (When the madness was at its height, most major networks tried to lure us away from MTV. I told them to fuck off.) It was like Beatlemania, with everybody trying to find 'the next Beatles'. You can't do it.

Just like Beatlemania, Osbournemania changed the cultural climate. Its impact has been global. In years to come I'm sure students will examine the phenomenon. Well, for what it's worth, here's my view. I see us lying somewhere between the Waltons, the Simpsons and the Addams family. Different, however, in one crucial way. We were not invented. The key to our extraordinary success, why *The Osbournes* worked, was that we were real.

I don't regret it. So many doors opened for all of us, so many opportunities. Like I said before, the only person whose life didn't change was Ozzy. He still has a thriving musical career, and in November 2005 he and Sabbath were inducted into the Rock and Roll Hall of Fame in the UK, and the following March in America.

No one would ever deny that we were lucky. The time was right, and we – and to their credit MTV – recognised that. Through it we became amazingly famous, we had the time of our lives. But all the money we made went on lawyers and settling the cases.

Despite the lawsuits, I loved *The Osbournes* because, when it came down to it, it was real, and because it was something I had come up with. I had a good feeling that it would work (though I had no idea to what level). I try to follow my gut with these things, but sometimes I make a mistake. Sometimes I listen to my ego . . . or to the money being offered. And when I do that, it's almost always a mistake. The chat show I did in the US – that wasn't me. I should never have done it. I let my ego and the money sway me.

I made a similar mistake in spring 2006, and the experience taught me a lot about how ugly things can get when you come up against people who are really desperate for celebrity. In a way it was the perfect example of how crazy the whole celebrity thing has become. It left a bad taste in my mouth, and I learned a lot from it.

I was in LA when Simon Cowell called me with a proposition.

'Listen, darling,' he said, 'we're doing a celebrity *X-Factor* at the end of May. Do you wanna do it?'

'Sure,' I said. 'I'll do it.' I knew I would be in London for a concert Ozzy was doing at the Tower of London to celebrate thirty years of the Prince's Trust. Ozzfest was ready to roll and *The X-Factor* auditions for the third series weren't set to start till later in June.

A couple of weeks before we were due to start, the production company faxed me the list of who was on the show, and two names jumped out: James Hewitt and Rebecca Loos. And I'm like, You've got to be fucking joking.

James Hewitt is the one-time paramour of Princess Diana and Rebecca Loos is the one-time PA to David Beckham. Their joint claim to celebrity is that they not only said that they'd slept with people who were married, but they both sold their sad little stories and made huge amounts of money from them, and then they proceeded to milk their notoriety in whatever way they could, reality shows being the main route. Ms Loos's second claim to fame is that she masturbated a pig on television.

As soon as I saw their names I called one of the producers.

'I thought this was meant to be a fun, light-hearted thing where well-known people basically take the piss out of themselves and raise money for charity. These people are distasteful. How can you ever give them a lifeline? If they were drowning I wouldn't throw them a rubber duck.'

'It makes good TV.'

So what's new? Well, I thought, I've signed up. I'll do it and go home. That was the limit of my agenda. I didn't have any preconceived notions beyond that.

I arrive at the studio on the first day, and discover that *The X-Factor: Battle of the Stars* is nothing like *The X-Factor* itself. The producers have chosen everybody. They are a hand-picked bunch – no wild cards, no auditions, and the judges are told who they are having to mentor right from the start. Some of them could sing, some of them couldn't. A good mix, and plenty of interesting stories and personalities. At least I wasn't down to mentor the bands, which would have included Hewitt and Loos. Simon had been landed with *that* particular short straw. I was lucky, I had the England rugby player Matt Stevens, a gentle giant with a fabulous voice, Michelle Marsh, a former page-three glamour model but again a great voice and a lovely personality, and Nikki Sanderson from *Coronation Street*, who you couldn't help but fall in love with and who was another natural singer. So far, so good.

First thing I do is introduce myself to everybody – that first-day-at-work thing. So I walk into make-up and it's, 'Hi there, I'm Sharon . . . How are you, good to meet you', and so on, and instantly I could sense a weird atmosphere.

I recognised Rebecca Loos immediately, of course. Hardly surprising as her face and other body parts had been splashed across the tabloids ever since the appalling business of her alleged affair with David Beckham had titivated the country a year before. She was dressed in some kind of miniskirt with her tits hanging out. Not a warm person, not an endearing person. Ice. Everybody else was great, a good group of people. She was disgusting and horrible. As I drove back to Welders that night, I thought: What the fuck am I doing there with all the ugliness and negativity?

Just before show time the next day word came backstage that Ms Loos was refusing to wear underwear under her dress. No knickers, no bra. Seems she didn't want any Visible Panty Lines. Later she claimed that the dress was so short it showed her thong, so she thought it was better to go without. Faa-bulous.

God knows I am used to people using their sexuality to achieve their ends, but I had never come across anything as blatant as this. As the day wore on I watched her playing the producers, using all the sexy, vulnerable little airhead tricks she could think of and it was just gaggable. Again I thought: What the fuck am I doing? I'm a whore because I'm here for the money. And I'm sitting, watching this woman who said she slept with a married man and then sold her story. And I can think of a word for that. This is really nasty and horrible and tasteless.

As for James Hewitt, I felt sorry for him. He is so desperate. He kept coming up with all these royal stories that nobody was interested in. 'Do you want to hear this story about when Charles and I were at such-and-such polo match?' No. Everything was, 'When I was in the army . . . when I was playing polo with the Nabob of Thing.' Everything he said was a parody. Even his voice sounded like a parody. All he could do was talk about horses and shooting and the royals and the army. Nobody wanted to hear it.

One of the producers went into the dressing room, and Hewitt had a silver hip flask and he was drinking from it and the producer said, 'Oh! A tot of brandy?' And love's young dream looked ostentatiously down at his watch and said, 'Oh no, dear boy, a sherry.'

He's a royal groupie. As for what Diana saw in him, God only knows. But we've all been vulnerable; we've all been desperate for comfort.

So it's show time. Simon introduces the deadly duo, as they're his act. She's wearing a skimpy black dress that's like two bits of material someone has forgotten to pin together – like a slit-open silk bin bag – and it's all hanging out. The only innocent thing about her is her hair. It's in a ponytail. The song is 'Addicted To Love', a song I had always liked. Until now. I sit there shell-shocked thinking, I cannot believe how unpleasant this all is.

As they begin to prance around, lights flashing, all this money being spent on making them look good, I watch them and I think, Who the fuck are you? Both of you are traitors, both of you have used sex to get what you want, have told your stories for money, have no moral code to live by. You have hurt other people to get money. You are shameless.

And the performance itself is execrable. Neither of them can sing a note. I have heard some bad voices in the hundreds of hours I have spent listening to *X-Factor* hopefuls, but I can honestly say I have rarely heard anything as excruciating as that. If it was anybody else, it would be hilarious. It is not hilarious. It is nauseating. I could not have laughed if my life depended on it. At the end Kate Thornton, who is hosting the show, turns to me first as if she knows she has to defuse me in case I explode. Her eyes are glazed, as if they have just come out of the fridge.

I sit back in my chair and smile.

'A good choice of song for you two,' I say carefully. 'A very appropriate song for you to sing.' Nobody is sure how to take this. Then somebody in the audience gets it and starts to titter.

'You two have so much in common,' I say 'and it shows on stage.' Then I turn directly to the captain. 'Weren't you in the army?'

'Yes,' he says, still not sure how to take me. I go on smiling at the smug little shit. 'Well, for that performance you should be shot.'

Now I turn my attention to her, smiling all the way. 'And you, missus. You know what? If you get through tonight you should try doing tomorrow's performance with your knickers on because it will help warm up your voice.' Behind me I hear the audience gasp, and to my right a groan from Louis.

I had planned none of it. It just came out.

Out of the corner of my eye I can see Simon moving his head, trying to protest, saying something about it being a family show. I take no notice. My eyes are locked on hers. It's as if we are the only two people in the room. She says something about not expecting me to say anything nice, that I had completely shunned her throughout the show. Too damned right I had. 'You've got a very bad vibe that comes from you,' I counter. 'I don't know what it is, it's very hostile.' Louis then jumps in to defuse the situation, saying that she looked great. I nodded, but I hadn't quite finished. 'You've got nice boobs,' I added. 'You've got a good boob job.'

'Look, Sharon,' she says, 'we're doing this for charity.'

'Your own charity.'

They were voted to stay on. The next day the press said it was because the public felt sorry for them after I had slated them. I like to think it was because the public wanted the abuse to continue.

I came off the set that night feeling as if I was the one who'd been abused. I had a horrible taste in my mouth. Not because of what I had said, but because of how people like this were being given a platform, were being paid for having betrayed people that had trusted them.

After the show, Simon came to find me in my dressing room. He was furious. 'I'm not interested in your personal view,' he said. 'These people have been invited here as guests of mine and I don't want you to disrespect them. You cannot treat people in that way.'

The next day the Loos woman was on morning chat shows, laying into me. I was a bully, she said. Cheap and vulgar. Just like Victoria Beckham, I had no elegance and no class – apparently you only get that by being born with it, like she was. And who was I to attack her for having an affair with a married man when I had done the same thing myself? At least the man she'd fucked had been good-looking and healthy, she said.

Oh please, get a fucking brain cell. She's a prime example of a celebrity groupie and the lengths people will go to have celebrity rub off on them. Someone that doesn't have the talent to be a star in their own right, yet likes the perks of being in that world, likes being seen at the parties, cosying up to this name and that name – all that shit. I mean, ask yourself: why would you put yourself through that humiliation? It was worse than the public stocks in the Middle Ages. It was there in the original idea of a duet with Hewitt. Nothing to do with me. Every day of the week people are at it with married men, it's human nature.

I'm not proud of what I did. It's true that when I met Ozzy he was still married, but I certainly didn't go on TV and belittle Ozzy's wife, which is what Rebecca Loos has done.

She also said that the real reason I attacked her was because I didn't want to be kicked off the Beckham's party list. Puh-lease. Although we had been to their World Cup party the week before, I barely know Victoria. In fact, as far as I was concerned, this comment said far more about Ms Loos than it did about me, about what she thought was important. Did she really think that sort of thing bothered me – whether or not I got invited to this party or that party? Like I give a shit. I suppose in her mind that would be the worst thing – to be struck off a celebrity party list. How shallow is that?

Their performance on the second night of 'Baby, It's Cold Outside' was equally appalling. I began by apologising for not having commented previously on their singing. I made some vaguely derogatory remark to him, then said to her, 'Talking about going down, I thought you had something stuck in your throat.' The audience loved it. They had booed the pair when they came on stage and now they were cheering.

The morning appearances on national television became a daily event. This time she turned her attention to my family and how I had used them to make money for myself in *The Osbournes* and went on about the kids and their drug problems.

I know I have a mouth like a truck driver but I also have this very simplistic view on life and the way to treat people and the way people treat me. You're nice to me, I'm nice to you. You're not, and I'll bite your head off. I've got to the age now where I don't have to pretend, I don't have to be a fake.

That was when I went to the producers and said, 'OK. It may be funny for you, great viewing figures for you, but there are other people that get hurt from the fall-out.'

117

I was to blame because I should never have done it. Nothing to do with what I said – I mean doing the show in the first place. The moment I saw their names I should have pulled out. My grandmother, Nana, my father's mother, used to say: 'If you can't say anything nice, don't say anything at all.' And so I took her advice. For the rest of the show I didn't ever comment on their performance. Neither of them have like-ability, neither of them have any talent to offer. They're just liggers.

At the end of the day, I learned a lot from what was really a nasty experience, and it gave me a very good lesson on the flipside of celebrity. In the end Matt Stevens was the runner-up, and a lovely actress called Lucy Benjamin who had been in *EastEnders* was voted the winner. Neither of them had been looking to become famous just for the sake of it. They weren't desperate to be celebrities. In fact, Lucy Benjamin looked terrified pretty much every time she got on stage, and hardly believed us when we told her how well she was doing. The contrast couldn't have been clearer. They had both done the show for the right reasons – to have a bit of fun and to make some money for charity. They could both sing.

And, as far as I know, they both kept their knickers on.

# Hollywood

'The flipside of celebrity.' My father had wanted to be famous as a young man. He had the most amazing voice. But it wasn't through his voice that he found fame. It was through his entrepreneurial skills, which made him infamous. And how people would describe him in the press. Don Arden – the infamous rock manager. He loved that – loved his reputation.

The whole episode with Ms Loos had been a cautionary tale for me on the more unpleasant side of modern celebrity. But it can be a lot worse. These days fame attracts all sorts of unwanted attention. And some of it can be very dangerous. Very scary.

I first heard the Beatles in 1963. I might have heard them a year earlier if my father had had the wit to say yes when John Lennon asked him to take on their management. John idolised Gene Vincent, who he knew my father managed, and in 1962 the Fab Four were playing at the Star Club in Hamburg where Don was in partnership with Manfred Weissleder, the club's owner. But my father didn't see any future in English rock and roll. It had to be American or nothing. So he turned them down.

Don had bought a portable record player for use at home. I remember it clearly. It was green and it came from Boots the chemist. You could stack up 45s and they would drop down one by one, and one of the first records I bought with my own money was 'Please, Please Me'.

In England in the early sixties, when it came to pop stars you had to take sides. Tommy Steele or Cliff Richard – you couldn't like both. Billy Fury or Adam Faith. Paul McCartney or John Lennon. Those were the rules. John Lennon was always the one for me.

The rise of the Beatles paralleled my adolescence. I grew up with them. Everyone was talking about them, young and old. For the first time young people mattered.

John Lennon was my chosen idol for the simple reason that we had the same birthday, 9 October. I was in love with him. It was a true passion, really strong, and I knew that he was going to marry me. How could he not when we shared the same birthday? It was fate, it was destiny. He knew that I knew that he knew. He only had to meet me . . .

I would write him letters all the time, but never got round to posting them. I'd hide them in the top left-hand drawer in my bedroom with my mascara and Max Factor Pan Stick that I thought nobody knew about. The letters were all very innocent, all about how gorgeous I thought he was. 'I love your singing . . . I love your hair . . . I love your suits.' And then my mother and brother found them and made fun of me, and that was the end of that.

One of my greatest regrets is that I never saw the Beatles perform live. I suppose I was just a bit too young. I did meet them, several years later: bumped into them all in fact, one day with my father on the pavement outside the Apple offices in Savile Row, which was only a couple of hundred yards from where we lived in Mayfair on Hay Hill.

Ozzy always cites the Beatles as his greatest influence. They were the catalyst, he says, that got him into music. And his version of 'In My Life' will always have a special resonance for me because it's the soundtrack to the collage of my life, the video that Ozzy made to accompany the single he did in 2005.

Everyone of my generation remembers where they were on the day John Lennon died. On 8 December 1980, Ozzy and I were in England. We were involved, but secretly – we were in the full flush of our romance. Although we had known each other for years, we had first slept together only a couple of months before. Ozzy was rehearsing in Monmouth for the second album, while I was in Wimbledon at my parents' house. I was on my own when I heard the news, in the bedroom I'd had since the family had moved there ten or so years earlier, and it was still the same as it had always been – pink wallpaper, a little girl's room. A newsflash came on the TV. The first thing I did was call Ozzy and I think we must have spoken for five hours on the phone that night. Both of us had been watching the TV at the same time and both of us were in a state of shock, as was the rest of the world. However weird it seems, when someone has been such a huge part of your life, even if you don't personally know them, it affects you just as much as if you'd been friends in reality. It leaves a huge gap. Just like Princess Diana's death did for so many people nearly twenty years later.

John Lennon had been my great idol. The Beatles had written the soundtrack to my life and to Ozzy's. John Lennon was the voice of our generation. He was the one who questioned everything, and in doing so allowed us to question everything. He was our hero.

And somebody killed him just to be famous.

# 5

---

# The Dark Side of Fame

I have always been a huge fan of Liza Minnelli. I have seen her every movie, every one of her one-woman shows, and I just adore her. It was a dream come true when she appeared on my chat show in the UK. Then, just a couple of nights later, we met again when we did *Parkinson* together. That night she had been very funny about the price of fame, and how it's always when a new date is in the middle of telling her some fabulous story that a fan will come over and stop him mid-flow and the moment will be lost.

While it's true that it's not necessarily what you feel like doing, I have always told Ozzy that the day people stop asking for your autograph is the day you have to worry, because your career is over. It doesn't harm anyone to be nice. And that kind of fan support is lovely. Just as I had worshipped John Lennon and adored Liza herself – it's a totally innocent thing.

For most of our married life no one was interested in the overweight woman by Ozzy's side. After *The Osbournes* all that changed, and the fame game now is played under totally different rules from when I was growing up. Then I was a kid with an autograph book getting signatures from people like Johnny Ray and Little Richard and Chuck Berry. It's not just your autograph that people want today, but your picture too, preferably with your arm around them.

Not everyone can turn up at a show or happen to catch you in a restaurant, so they still write in for pictures and, just as I have always done for Ozzy, I get the office to send a signed photograph. At the end of the day, it's flattering that you mean something to someone; it can stop at any time and I always remember that.

Ever since the second series of *The X-Factor*, I had been getting letters from a small group of fans that seemed to communicate with each other through the internet, and that had no other connection except their interest in me.

Then one night in April 2006, when I was performing in the show *The Vagina Monologues* – in Southampton, I think it was – among the fans waiting at the stage door was a woman who thanked me for the signed photo I had sent her. She told me her name, explained that she had written me a letter, in fact several letters, but that she was so happy to have met me in person. She told me where she was from, and I remember being vaguely aware that she must have come a long way. So I smiled and scrawled my signature on the front of her programme: 'To Doreen, I love you, Sharon'. She was very nice and very respectful and I didn't think any more about it.

Then letters from this same group began arriving at Welders. Not in the post, but put by hand in the letterbox at the gatehouse. You could see from the addresses that these people didn't live locally, and I realised they must have made special journeys to get to the house.

The next time I was aware of them was at my chat show, which was filmed at the London Weekend Television studios on the South Bank. It was recorded either a day or two days before it went out, to allow the editors to tidy it up a bit yet still remain topical.

After each recording I would go down into the audience and shake everyone's hand – have photos taken and sign autographs and copies of my book, which by now was out in paperback. Until then the only member of this group I had met was Doreen. But then others began identifying themselves, telling me that their name was such-and-such and they were the ones who'd been writing to me for a year. So I'd say, 'Oh great, great!' And whether I wanted to or not, I began to put faces to the names. So OK. Then they'd be there the next day, and the next. Each time they'd want to see me and shake my hand and have their picture taken with me. They'd bring me gifts. Scarves and flowers. Things they'd clearly taken trouble with and spent money on.

This went on day after day, and I began to feel uneasy about it. Talkback, the production company making the show, agreed, and it was decided to limit the number of times individuals could come to the show to twice. Two shows. But they still kept coming – they must have got ticket allocations under false names.

Then one day one of them calls me at home.

'How did you get my number?' I asked after the preliminaries were done.

'Oh, I got it off the internet.'

Immediately I had the number changed.

A few weeks later it happened again. I changed it again.

Then Kelly got a phone call at her house. Omar, a friend she had staying, picked up the phone.

'Can I speak with Kelly?' says the caller.

'She's not here.'

'Oh. You must be Omar. You live with Kelly, don't you? I'm actually looking for Sharon. Is she there?'

Now, nobody knows about Omar. He's never mentioned in the press, never mentioned on my shows. He's just a friend. The phone call scares him, so he calls me. Now I'm scared too. If they know about Omar, and they have the number of the house, chances are they have the address. So then we change Kelly's number.

Next up is Gary Farrow, our publicist in England. Gary had appeared a few times on *The X-Factor*, and he helped me pick some of the people I was going to mentor. So now he gets a call. This time it's not a landline, it's his mobile.

'Where is Sharon today? What is she doing? Is she with Kelly? What is she doing next week?'

And Gary just goes, 'What the fuck is it to do with you? Fuck off!'

Now Gary's mobile is his lifeline. With the client list he has, he cannot change the number. But as he wasn't giving them the answers they wanted, they began to pester. One day he got fifty-two phone calls. Anyone else can switch their phone off, but he can't. Their next game was to record his answers and play them back to him, him fucking around, screaming down the phone, swearing at them.

On 8 September, a week or so into the show, the head office of ITV in Birmingham received a bomb threat. The caller said something was going to happen at the show within the next ten minutes. The eighth of September was a Friday and although it was on air at the time of the call, the caller obviously didn't realise that the show had been recorded two days before and the studio was empty. Shortly after this, the offices of Thames Television in London had a call from a woman claiming to be a police officer from Scotland Yard. The Talkback production office immediately called Scotland

Yard on another line and they said to check the caller's warrant number. This the caller obviously couldn't provide, and she hung up. What made it all the stranger was that the caller at one point put the call on hold and there was the sound of a recorded message saying: 'You are being put through to New Scotland Yard's general enquiry number.' They had gone to a lot of trouble. The police went into Thames and took statements from everybody involved. I should say that I was oblivious to all this at the time. It was decided to keep it from me until they knew what was happening. It was only later that I saw the report.

Later that same evening the studio got another call, this time from a woman claiming to be in charge of the bomb-threat investigation at Scotland Yard. She demanded my phone number, saying she needed to contact me urgently to check I was safe. She gave the real switchboard number for Scotland Yard but a false extension. As the report on it later said: 'It is now beginning to look like a very elaborate plot to extract contact details for Sharon Osbourne. What's odd is that the caller is extremely persistent and forceful. If we weren't as cynical as we are, she would have convinced someone very quickly that she was genuine. She knew the police had been here as she'd been told that by security downstairs. She expressed outrage that she hadn't authorised any officers to attend.'

We still don't know if this bomb hoax had any connection with the other group. What I do know is that it freaked me out.

I would arrive at a charity reception and there would always be a couple of familiar faces that had turned up at all my public events. Or I'd be coming out and one of them would grab hold of my arm and say, 'Where have you been? I've been waiting here for three hours. Why did you go in by another entrance?' And I'm like, What the fuck are you doing here, anyway? I'm attending a charity dinner or event, I didn't ask you to come, what are you doing here?

Someone said that it's not really that different from the way Tony Dennis, Ozzy's long-term assistant, came into our lives over twenty-five years ago. I'm sorry, but it's entirely different. These women were in their thirties and forties. Tony Dennis and his friend were sixteen years old when Ozzy and I first met them, during the first UK tour in 1980. They were innocent young fans who hero-worshipped Ozzy. They would never have dreamed of stepping over the line. Tony didn't think that because he bought Ozzy's records he had bought a piece of his life.

There was a man standing outside Welders one time, blocking the way, and as we slowed down he held up a stack of records and said through the window, 'Would Ozzy sign these?' And I'm like, No, no, no! First of all this is a narrow lane and we're not going to pull up, and second, you're not going to come beyond the gate. This is our home, our sanctuary. I said, 'No, Ozzy's not signing them.' And I thought: You don't come to somebody's house like that and then ambush them. It's just not on.

Then he began to turn aggressive. 'But I bought you this house, people like me bought you this house. I bought all your records.'

So I said to Tony, who was driving, 'Give him a couple of hundred quid. Give him his money back.' And Tony did.

By mid-October the chat show was over and we were into live shows at *The X-Factor*, and this guy, the only man in the 'group', starts turning up at the stage door on a regular basis. Sign this, sign that. Occasionally he had flowers. Pushy but basically nice. Nothing you could really take exception to.

So we're getting well into *The X-Factor* – the last few shows before Christmas 2006 – when Gary gets a phone call from Kelly in tears. I've taken an overdose, I'm high, I need my mum, I can't remember my mum's phone number. Gary, give me my mum's phone number. And he calls me immediately. It's gone midnight.

'Sharon. Gary. I've just had a call from Kelly. She's in a bad way.' And then he begins to take me through the hysterical phone call he's just had. He'd barely started when I told him to stop.

'She's not in a bad way, Gary. I know exactly where she is and she's absolutely fine.'

There was a beat of silence the other end, then a groan and 'Fuck.'

Gary had given this caller my cell-phone number. He didn't know it was a hoax.

I wait. The phone starts going about one in the morning. Private number. It could be someone I know, but nobody in my index. It rings on and off for two hours. I pick it up at around three.

'Hello?'

'Aren't you angry I've got your number?'

'No. Not remotely. What do you want? I'll talk to you.'

It was a guy. I don't know if it was the guy from *The X-Factor*, but his voice did seem familiar. Either way, I knew things weren't right.

'Who are you with?'

'What do you mean, who am I with?'

'Who are you lying in bed with?'

Very confident, but jabbing. Accusatory. Meanwhile, I made my voice light. 'No one,' I said.

'Where's your famous anger then? Where's your big Sharon Osbourne rant? Why aren't you angry that I've got your number?'

'I'm not angry all the time, you know. I'm awake. I'll talk. What do you want to talk to me about?'

'I told you. Who's with you? Who's lying next to you?'

'Minnie. I'm here with Minnie.'

'Why aren't you asleep?

'I don't sleep a lot.'

'Why aren't you angry with me?'

'Can't be bothered.' On and on it went in circles. Why don't you sleep? Why are you still up? What are you going to do tomorrow? What are you doing next week? Which house are you in? Where is your bed?

I guessed he was recording it – there were little clicks on the line, and Gary's experience had taught me that. It was one reason I'd decided to play it the way I had. Eventually I said, 'You're recording this telephone call, aren't you?'

'No, no. Why would I want to do that?'

'I know who you are. I've met you at *The X-Factor*.'

'No you haven't.'

'Oh yes I have. Look,' I said, 'it's not a problem. Any time you want to call me, just call.' And finally, after about forty-five minutes, he got bored. Of course, the instant he hung up, I called the phone company and changed the number.

Then shortly after this a letter arrived at Welders, hand-delivered to the box at the gatehouse, from Doreen. She had booked herself in a hotel down the road, she told me, gave me the number and said, 'I'm here and I'm waiting for you to call.'

By now I felt real concern for this woman. In the end we are all human. So I decided to call her up and find out what she wanted from me.

She didn't seem that surprised to hear from me. She told me she knew I would call, and that she knew we were going to be best friends. She had dreamed of us spending time together, and that she would become an integral part of my life. She said if I needed an assistant she would love to help out, as she knew I must be overwhelmed with my workload. And she was a professional working woman.

She was the last person I'd want as my PA. My response was, Doreen, you have a job, and I have an assistant. We're not going to be best friends, you're not going to be part of my life. Get on with your *own* life.

On 7 November, a finalist from the previous year of *The X-Factor*, Andy Abraham, had a solo concert at the Albert Hall and I wouldn't have missed it for the world. I was in a box up at the back of the auditorium, directly facing the stage, and when I came in the people in the audience got up and clapped, which was lovely and very touching. I was so pleased for Andy. He is the sort of person who makes *The X-Factor* worthwhile. Before he auditioned he was a dustman and he is a sweet guy with a wonderful voice and personality. He could so easily have won, but he lost out to Shayne Ward by a tiny percentage of the vote. I was just pleased I had been able to help him on his way.

During the interval I went to the bathroom, as you do, and was just coming out of the cubicle when somebody blocked my way. I looked up. Doreen. My heart dropped straight into my stomach I don't know what I thought – I just felt fear. I walked straight past her and practically ran back to the box and shut the door behind me. But she had gone.

The night of *The X-Factor* wrap party, which is always held a couple of days after the finals are over, clashed with a private screening of my movie debut, *It's a Boy Girl Thing*. David

Furnish, Elton's long-time partner, had come across the film script and decided to make it. It was basically about a girl and a boy who live next door to each other and something sci-fi happens and they wake up one morning having swapped bodies. All very innocent and fun. The boy's mother is loud and brash and pushy, so when David and Elton were casting there was one person that came immediately to mind. It only involved a couple of days' filming in Canada and then a couple of days in the studio in London, and I couldn't resist it. My first movie, and I was working with two of my favourite people in the world. And it wasn't a stretch for me. And I would never have missed the screening of my first movie. Faa-bulous!

Conveniently both events were being held in Leicester Square on the same night. Kelly came with me to the movie screening first, and then to the cocktail party afterwards. As we were leaving to go over to *The X-Factor* party, she grabbed my arm.

'Oh my God, Mum,' she hissed. 'Run for the car. Doreen's here!' I looked across and there she was, with her eyes shining through the crowd, caught in the flash of the paparazzi's cameras. I could barely see her – when they flash you at night it really impairs your vision. Usually at events like this I take my time, sign a few autographs – after all, these people have waited a good while – but Kelly and security were pulling me towards the car. All I could see in my mind was Doreen's crazed eyes and the white frothy saliva that was always there at the corners of her mouth.

We quickly made for the car. Although *The X-Factor* party was just the other side of the square, no way could you walk through those kinds of crowds. It was packed, not only with fans, but the mass of tourists and theatregoers that are always milling around, like any other night.

*The X-Factor* party is always a laugh. It's one of the only times you get to have a drink with the crew, and all twelve finalists are invited. Kelly and I had a great night. We were there for a good couple of hours before I asked my security guard to call the car to wait for us out front. As he led the way through the crowd to get us safely delivered, suddenly from nowhere my arm was grabbed and wrenched, and at the same time I heard my name being screamed in my face. 'Sharon! Sharon!' Doreen was back, tugging at my arm. My heart was pounding – she was hurting me, the sheer strength of her hands – and I'm not a weak woman, I'm strong, but she was really pulling on me and a few stands of her long black hair had got caught in one of my rings. Security tried to get her off, but she wouldn't let go and her nails were digging in my arm. It's a fine line security have to tread, as they could be done for assault, if she wanted to play that game.

It was such a downer after such a great evening. *The X-Factor* party had been a celebration of another successful series. But coming out and being met by Doreen, I just thought – Why me? It was such a reminder of the price you pay for celebrity. And it wouldn't be the last time I saw her.

At the beginning of January 2007 I was back in Doheny in LA, preparing for my operations and supporting Ozzy as he worked on his new album. One morning Melinda came running upstairs to my bedroom to say there was a woman hanging around outside the house. I quickly put on a wrap and went down to the garage – where security have the CCTV monitors – and took a look.

'It's her,' I said, peering over their heads. And there she was: Doreen, sitting on the steps leading up to the pedestrian gate. I couldn't believe it.

In Beverly Hills there's a local by-law that says you cannot loiter. You cannot sit outside somebody's house like that. Legally you have to move on. So Perkins, one of our security guards, went out, and gave it to her straight: 'Excuse me, ma'am, you are loitering, it's against the law and you gotta move on.' So she went, and I breathed a huge sign of relief.

Next day I was in my car with Melinda. We were both in the front and she was driving, and we had stopped at a cross-roads, as you have to in Beverly Hills, where nobody has right of way and it's like a slow waltz with cars stopping and starting all the time at every intersection they come to, when suddenly she clutches my hand and hisses, 'OH MY GOD!' And there she was: Doreen. Walking across the road in front of us. Fortunately she was staring straight ahead and didn't see us, and we drove back as quickly as we could as she was clearly walking up Doheny Road.

She had delivered a letter. Melinda opened it and read it while I unpacked the groceries. She was in LA, she said. Then stuff about how much money she had laid out to buy the ticket. That she'd be coming back to the house at four and she would love to have a chat.

She arrived bang on four. Perkins went out and said, 'Sorry, ma'am, you are not coming in. You gotta go, you gotta move on.'

'But I've arranged to see Sharon.'

'There's nobody home.'

'Please give her this letter.'

'I'll put it on the pile.'

'What do you mean, the pile?'

'There's a huge pile of letters.'

'Will she read my letter?'

'I couldn't say. I do my job. I put it on the pile of letters and that's what I do. That's as far as it goes.'

Then she began to get nasty. 'But she said she was my friend! How can she be my friend if she doesn't read my letters?'

She was there for four days and then she left.

Eventually a letter arrived in the post from England. She wrote to say how she had gone to all the places I'd written about in my book. She'd gone to the Beverly Hills Hotel, to Kay's salon, to the house in Belair, to Benedict Canyon looking for the Howard Hughes house, to Sunset, to Venice Beach, to Malibu – she'd even tried to find my father's rest home off Hollywood Boulevard. All the places where I'd been, as if she were following some surreal Sharon Osbourne heritage trail. She ended up:

'So I know now that I could never be your friend because I can never live this lifestyle so we don't have anything in common.'

Of course I never encouraged her to think she could be my friend. The problem is, if they call out, 'I love you,' and you call out, 'I love you too,' some people take it literally.

There are always people who cross the line – who think they own you. That you owe them. But I don't let it worry me too much – I can take care of myself.

# Hollywood

It's so strange to think of Doreen trying to hunt down my father's nursing home. Thank God she didn't find it. I'm sure the staff wouldn't have let her past the door, but even so. As if my father doesn't have enough problems. Doreen would definitely have had a one-way conversation.

I take his hand again. No response. Would it be any different if I visited every day? I don't think so. Dari visits regularly and there's no recognition there either.

Poor Dari – she's such a godsend, but she has her own troubles at the moment. Just a few weeks ago she heard that her mother had died back in Georgia. She was unable to go to the funeral because she can't leave America as she still doesn't have a passport. She was devastated.

I have to make a decision about Don's funeral before it's too late. I've left a message with Gina to ask her mother, my half-sister Dixie. See if they can shed any light on what he would have wanted. It's all such a mess.

When my mother died she was estranged from Don, though not divorced. She would never have allowed that. He was living permanently with his mistress, Meredith, in Los Angeles. The odd thing was that my mother was buried in a double plot in a churchyard in Surrey, near Dorking, under the North Downs. Nobody knows whose decision that was. Hers or Don's. Now we need to know. Does he want to be buried beside her? She was a Catholic and my father is Jewish, so there's even more of a complication there. Yet it has to be decided now, because in the Jewish religion the body is not embalmed and you have to be buried within twenty-four hours of death.

Where would he want to be buried? I have these conversations with myself at night. My instinct is that he would want to go to a Jewish cemetery in Manchester, where his mother is buried and where his sister Eileen still lives.

One thing I do know is that he truly loves his religion. He has always been proud to be a Jew. But I would have to bring him back to England. I couldn't bury him here in California all alone.

OK. Don has to be buried in England. I have to fly him back. Bloody hell – where do I begin with that one?

Who would I call in Manchester to help with the arrangements? I'd have to call Auntie Eileen, who I haven't spoken to in a few years. That in itself will be awkward, but I know she's the only one who can help. I'm not versed in the Jewish religion. I don't know what the procedure is. I don't know anything. Eileen is old now, older than Don, but she still works at the *shul* where Don went, and where he first sang.

It's strange to be sitting here with my father still alive, thinking about these things. But I know something has to be done. I just wish I wasn't the one who had to make the decision. It's so ironic. For years my father cut me out of his life. No one was to speak of me. In his eyes I was dead. But now, here at the end, I'm left with this decision. It's not what I wanted, but I have to take responsibility for him. I just wish I knew what he wanted. If he would only give me a sign.

Maybe Manchester is the right place? That's where he was born eighty-one years ago. Harry Levy. He changed his name because there was so much anti-Semitism around at the time. It was in Manchester where he got his first taste of show business. First and foremost, Don was a performer. He loved to sing, tell jokes. He used to do impersonations – Al Jolson, Frank Sinatra.

It's in my blood, too. I love performing. When I was a kid, the performances were often put on for my father's benefit. One of my earliest memories is being sent to answer the door when the bailiffs came round, to say my parents weren't in. I was just a kid – maybe eight or nine years old. Once the bailiffs had gone I would head for the kitchen downstairs where my 'audience' was waiting – Don and my mother, laughing their heads off. 'Shah showed them, didn't she, she got rid of the fuckers.'

Ozzy says his mum used to ask him to do the same thing when he was little. She'd buy things from the tallyman and he'd come round for payment. She would say, 'Tell him I'm not in', and Ozzy would go to the door and say, 'My mum says she's not in'. Bless him. As for me, I got the attention, I got the approval. Big time. Right from the start, I learned to play a role.

But I have to say it wasn't all bad. I learned so much from my father. He loved the stage, loved performing and although I may not have become a dancer like everyone expected, I still love the theatre, and that's something I definitely got from both my parents. Going to see a show was something we did regularly as a family when I was growing up. It was one of the best gifts they gave me. In the last few years I've appeared on stage a few times and I've loved every minute of it.

# 6

---

# Performance

While the lawsuit against *The Osbournes* was painful right to the bitter end, another lawsuit had a happier outcome. In early 2005 I had agreed to take part in a production of *The Vagina Monologues* in London. What made the London offer particularly tempting was that Aimee would be doing it with me, and the one thing I do regret about *The Osbournes* is the time I lost with her, my firstborn. She decided right at the beginning that she didn't want to do it, didn't want to get involved at all. Those are three years I can never get back. So for me being able to work with her on this was a huge plus.

Then, shortly before rehearsals were about to begin, she got sick, and I made the decision that this was not the moment.

She had to go back to Los Angeles and I went with her. The production company sued me for breach of contract. A quarter of a million pounds. Not what they were going to have paid me, but the money they said they had lost by my not performing.

All my life I have had a horror of being sued. As a child, I was always having to fend off bailiffs and writ servers for my father. Yet here was another one to do my head in. It seemed never-ending.

It dragged on for nearly a year – figures flying to and fro across the Atlantic: how much the advertising had cost, how many people asked for refunds, how much was being given to charity, etc. – yet each side stood to lose thousands of pounds on legal fees whatever the eventual outcome. One morning I woke up and just thought: This is completely ridiculous. I had always wanted to do the show, so why didn't I just get off my arse and do it? Two weeks, I said. So long as it's not in London. They agreed: Newcastle and Southampton, the two extremities of the country. They didn't pay me, I didn't pay them.

Tim Sheader, the director, was fab and we hit it off immediately. He was reassuring and nurturing and helped me to develop the characters for each of the women whose words I was speaking. He was a lovely person to work with, and I will always be grateful to him for making the whole experience such a pleasure. It was also my luck to work with two wonderful professionals: Lisa Riley, who made her name in

*Emmerdale*, and has such an infectious sense of humour that you are in danger of collapsing with laughter whenever you're with her, and Jenny Jules, a terrific young theatre actress who shamed us all with her quiet dignity. If there's any justice in the world, she has a great career ahead of her.

Ozzy's assistant Tony comes from Newcastle and his brother Mark still lives there. So he took good care of my PA Silvana and me when we were up there. Silvana Arena is the best PA in the world. Possibly the universe. She's a friend of Melinda's from Melbourne. She's like the key to a car, the pilot light on a stove. Without her, nothing functions.

I also brought Jude as an extra security blanket – he has looked after my hair and make-up in LA ever since the day *The Osbournes* started filming.

This trip wasn't Jude's first time in England, but it was his first time in Geordie-land. Lisa and Jenny adored him as girls always do, and every night after we'd eaten, the four of them (Silvana went too) would go clubbing. London is one thing, but for a six-foot-four Angelino who looks like an Apache, Newcastle was something else. He couldn't believe the culture and the next day he'd regale me with stories of drunken girls littering the streets.

'Sha-rone, you wouldn't believe it. They fall over in front of you! You see them passed out in shop doorways! And those skimpy clothes, you'd think they were in Miami!' As for the drinking – comparatively speaking, he said, he was like a fully paid-up member of AA.

The first night could have been a disaster. Naturally I was terrified. TV I can do. There's always the knowledge that if you fuck up you can do it again, and audiences of millions don't bother me. But eight hundred women in a theatre? That was scary. I don't think I have ever been so nervous and I piddled the day away, my heart hammering.

Somebody suggested 'drama drops' as the thing to calm the butterflies in my tummy. I had never heard of them. But about an hour before curtain up, Silvana came back with something called Rescue Remedy, the official name. It was a small brown bottle with a dropper and a rubber bulb on top. You put a couple of drops on your tongue and all nerves disappear. That, at any rate, was the idea. So I put a couple of drops on my tongue, waited a few minutes, but nothing happened. The hammering heart just kept on hammering. So I did another few drops. Still nothing. Five minutes to go and I thought: What the fuck, and swigged the whole bloody lot. About a tablespoonful in total. And then I went on.

All three of us wore black. I usually wore a plain top and a long skirt, Lisa a trouser suit and Jenny a chic little dress. The set was simple, a blood-red floor cloth and three high stools in a line, with two tables between them for the cue cards and a bottle of water.

So the first night I climb onto my stool and the performance begins. Mine was the first of the monologues – all of them drawn from interviews that the author, Eve Ensler, did with women all over the world and from every culture. The piece is an exploration of women's sexuality.

So I do mine and it goes fine. Five minutes in, and I'm feeling so relaxed I can hardly believe I ever worried about it. Lisa is doing her piece and for the first time I see how incredibly funny it is, and start laughing and laughing. Suddenly there's a crash, and I am on the floor, helpless with laughter.

By now the audience is laughing too, but the girls are looking aghast and the stage manager is glaring at me from the wings, making 'get-up' signs with her hands.

'I'm pissed,' I announce through the giggles, somehow managing to stagger up. Then 'Fuck it,' as I try a couple of times to clamber back onto the stool. 'Excuse me,' I said by way of explanation to the audience. 'But you see I'm pissed!'

And I was. Everyone thought I'd been on the bottle but I hadn't had a drink for days. It was the drama drops. I don't know what effect the herbs had, but the alcohol they'd been soaked in worked brilliantly. I was banned from ever using them again.

One of the recurrent themes was orgasm, and in one of my monologues, I had to build to an orgasmic climax. I am not an actress and I hardly ever did anything the same way twice. So one night I was sitting there on the stool, making all the noises, and building and building when, without knowing what I was doing, I slipped off the stool onto the floor, pulled my skirt up over my head, and grabbing my bottle of Evian, threw water all over my crotch before again collapsing in hysterical laughter, though this time everyone else joined in.

Doing the orgasm shtick was always a bit of a problem. The stage direction in one particular monologue of mine was very specific. Machine Gun. I had to make a noise like a machine gun to represent orgasm. Naturally Tim, the director, wanted me to do it in rehearsals – it was in the script – but I couldn't. 'Trust me,' I said. 'I just need to work on it. It'll be all right on the night.'

Kelly had come up to support her mum for the opening and we were going through my lines together in the dressing room, but every time I came to the machine-gun bit, I stopped. I could not do it. So she and Jude were coming up with various suggestions. Kelly suggested an erg-erg-erg-erg stuttering kind of noise.

I tried. No good.

Finally she had to leave to get to her seat. That left Jude.

'What am I going to do, Jude? I can't make a noise like a fucking machine gun. I just can't!'

'Yes you can, Sha-rone. Just take a deep breath and go rat-a-tat-tat.'

'Rat-a-tat-tat? Are you sure?'

'Sure I'm sure. Trust me. I'm a man. I know the noise. Rat-a-tat-tat.'

So that's what I did.

The moment comes, I'm feeling very confident. I feel as if I've just had Robert De Niro give me a master class in method acting. Here I am, I am a machine gun, ready to give an orgasm.

'Rat-a-tat-tat!'

I did it superbly.

Sadly, not everybody thought so.

There was silence, then I heard one of the girls snorting.

After the show the director came into the dressing room.

'You sounded like Kenneth Williams,' Tim said. He was furious. 'What the fuck did you think that was?'

'Rat-a-tat-tat!'

He looked at me as if he had just entered another universe.

'But rat-a-tat-tat is the sound a door knocker makes!'

In Newcastle perhaps. Not in Hollywood . . .

Every show we laughed. Every show was sold out, and it has to be said that it's a great feeling when you go out there on stage knowing there isn't an empty seat in the house. At the end I was so hooked that I was down there waiting in the wings before the others had even left their dressing rooms, so desperate was I to get out on stage. There was such warmth out there, both from the audience and Lisa and Jenny, and I ended up loving it. When I finish TV stuff, it's over, gone, forget about it. But this was different. I miss it and I would definitely do it again, if offered the chance.

Sticking to a script is not something I am famous for, and I never went out there word-perfect, though I always had the cue cards and sometimes would end up reading from them. Nobody seemed to mind. When I lost my place, which I often did, I would just go Fuck Shit Bollocks, then either I would find my place again or one of the girls would help.

There was an interdependence between the three of us that I had never experienced in television. When an actor is on stage and something unexpected happens, you've only got one another to bail you out. There's a danger in that, but it's a creative danger.

One night, we're in Southampton, right in the middle of one of my monologues, and I watch this woman walk from the back of the stalls down to the front of the stage, then plonk her arse on the edge of the orchestra pit. She was about forty-five, wearing a silk blouse and a nice cardigan. A bit like Helen Mirren in *The Queen*. Very prim and proper. And then she begins to shout.

'I read Eve Ensler's book,' she yells, loud enough for me to have to stop. 'I didn't buy a ticket to hear you read it.'

'Then what the fuck are you doing here?' I said, to a ripple of laughter. I loved being heckled; I'm like, Bring it on!

'Because I thought you were going to tell me how you masturbate and how you orgasm.'

The laughter had stopped. I pulled the microphone closer to my mouth.

'What did you say?'

'I want you to tell me how you all masturbate. I want you to teach me.'

Out of the corner of my eye I saw Lisa and Jenny sitting bolt upright, their eyes locked on me, like deer caught in the headlights.

'Look here, missus. You wanna know how to masturbate? This is how every woman masturbates.' Then I lifted up my finger, licked it, and shoved it between my legs. 'Now, fuck off!'

Kelly came up to the first night in Newcastle; Aimee and Ozzy made it to the last night in Southampton. Jack refused point-blank to have anything to do with it. He had seen the script, he said, and listening to his mother going on about her vagina for two hours was not his idea of fun. And I get that. I know that Ozzy didn't really want to come either, but I was really happy that he was there, gritted teeth or not. Even Tony braved the massed women so that Ozzy wasn't the only man in the audience. I suppose it was self-ish of me, but I was proud of what I had achieved and wanted to share it with the people who matter to me most. But it's fair to say it's probably for the best that my son *didn't* see me . . .

It had all been such an unexpected pleasure, and I think I was on a bit of a high from it. But my next show didn't play to my strengths the way *The Vagina Monologues* did. It taught me that valuable lesson: Never let your ego, or a fat pay cheque, persuade you to do something that your instinct tells you to isn't right.

In April 2006, just after I had finished *The Vagina Monologues* in Southampton, I made a pilot for a chat show with Simon Cowell's production company, Syco. The 2005 season of *The X-Factor* had gone well – Mrs . had behaved herself and the viewing figures had gone up and up – and, although the American chat show I'd done throughout 2004 had never taken off, Simon convinced me that England would be another story.

The pilot was a hoot. Like the show Simon proposed, it was just under an hour long. Graham Norton and Shayne Ward were my guests, with Ozzy's sisters doing an outside broadcast. I have always got on well with Ozzy's sisters – who on this occasion were dubbed 'The Ozzettes' – and I think and hope they had a fun time. They did a red-carpet inter-view piece at the first night of a West End play called *Smaller* starring Dawn French and Alison Moyet. They did it prop-erly – staying in a swanky hotel, getting full hair and make-up, meeting Jools Holland and Lenny Henry, who was there to support his wife, Dawn.

Making a pilot is an expensive business, and I was deter-mined not to let Simon down and to be at my most relaxed and confident, so I surrounded myself with people I felt com-fortable with. Shayne Ward had won *The X-Factor* the previous year, and it was great to see him doing well.

As always with Graham Norton, we had a blast. He had his

gorgeous young puppy with him, though not as well behaved as Minnie. We did a thing on celebrity perfumes – there had suddenly been a spate of them. I'd brought on samples of David Beckham's, Paris Hilton's and Jade Goody's, and the pair of us were soon cackling away like a couple of old queens. Jade Goody's, Graham decided, smelled 'Like a hot day in Hastings. Fish and chips'. Frankly I wouldn't have been so kind. The only perfume that either of us would have paid money for was David Beckham's. I wonder why . . .

We shot the pilot in front of a specially invited audience one evening, and it was funny and it was naughty. ITV loved it and took it.

It was all a gigantic mistake. I should never have agreed to do it, not the series, not even the pilot. I had been given a hard lesson when I did a chat show in America, but I hadn't learned. My ego had got the better of me.

I was booked to do forty shows. Eight weeks, five a week, each an hour long. We shot one on Sundays, two on Mondays and two on Tuesdays. A gruelling schedule, however you look at it. The pilot had been a doddle compared with what followed.

This was daytime TV, and a lot of my guests were from soap operas and I haven't watched a soap opera in thirty years. So I had a lot of catching up to do. I spent hours learning all the storylines. In addition, I had to be so careful with what I said and how I said it. No swearing, nothing too provocative.

Minnie did her best to bring a little light-heartedness into the proceedings by biting the guests – aided by my scattering flakes of chicken on the sofa before they sat down – but even with her around it was hard work.

I love meeting people. I'm in the people business. I don't sell chocolate or cars or tins of beans. I'm fascinated by the way we all live. Because I don't represent a particular class or a particular group, I feel just as comfortable at Buckingham Palace as I do at Ozzfest. Sometimes when you meet someone, what they are and what they represent is written all over them. I'm not like that. Even my accent is kind of mixed. It's not that I'm a chameleon, it's just that I don't belong to one particular group. I'm my own person.

But on daytime TV I just never came across that way. And it meant that from the moment I sat down on that sofa I was basically lost. The questions I really wanted to ask, I never could.

Did I ask David Beckham what he thought he was doing with that Loos woman? No. He was there to talk about his footballing book, and the camps he runs for young people. For the record I think he's a great guy who genuinely loves kids, but I didn't get to ask him what I really wanted.

Then there was Peter Andre, who is married to Jordan. He was promoting their record, so that's what we talked about, though I can't remember anything about it. What I would have liked to ask him was: Don't you think her tits are too big?

Another of my guests was Penny Lancaster, now the fourth Mrs Stewart. She was there to talk about a new book on photography, and I like photography. But what I would really like to have asked her was how hard she had found it dealing with the baggage that Rod brings to a relationship. Now that would have been an interesting discussion.

Then there was Rachel Hunter, the third Mrs Stewart. The obvious question there was: Why did you leave Rod? What was the final thing that pushed you over the edge?

That's not to say I never had any fun during the series. Julianne Moore had a naughty sense of humour, which I hadn't expected. When I told her Ozzy was a huge fan – which he is – she gave him a huge shout. Then there was Beyoncé, who I've known for several years. She had just done *Dream Girls* when I interviewed her, and she is such a gracious and beautiful woman, a good family girl, with a great mum and dad.

When people are truly talented and truly famous, the people around them don't go around saying: Don't ask her this, Don't ask her that, Call her Miss Beyoncé. Dealing with the ones that behaved like prima donnas when they were nothing of the sort made me want to scream.

The people I really enjoyed talking to, of course, were real stars and old friends. When the two were combined I was in heaven. I loved having Dita von Teese on the show. She is completely divine. She is the most exquisite woman, a burlesque dancer and a unique artist. I first got to know her about eight years ago when she began dating Marilyn Manson, who she later married. In 1998 she came and performed at Ozzy's fiftieth birthday party at the Beverly Hills Hotel.

The ultimate interview for me, the one that made the whole sorry exercise worthwhile, was when I got to meet Liza Minnelli. It could have been simply embarrassing, I could have been left speechless when faced with my idol, but we had this instant connection and within seconds it was as if we'd been friends all our lives. And then two days later she and I did that *Parkinson* show together and had the best time, gossiping like fishwives before we went on. Before I joined them on stage, she sang a song that I had never heard her sing – a song Charles Aznavour used to sing. It is sung for someone who is deaf, and ends with the performer signing as well as singing. She performed it sitting in a chair in a spotlight, that extraordinary face glowing with emotion and passion. It was such a moving performance and everyone was in tears, including me listening in the wings.

Parky asked her with great skill and humour how come she made such good choices in her professional life and such bad ones in her private life, spectacularly bad when it came to her last marriage to David Gest. While she was going through her divorce from David Gest I had my American chat show, and every day there was something in the news about it, how he claimed that she had hit him over the head and that he had to have Botox to kill the pain.

Listening to Michael doing the interview, apparently so effortlessly, I thought: That man, now, he knows how to do it. But for me it continued to be hard work, like pulling teeth. I felt like a piece of felt. Flat and boring. As the series went on, I did get better at making people feel comfortable enough to open up, but it takes confidence to do that.

The truth is that I'm crap at hosting daytime TV. I am not a daytime person. I did around 156 shows in America and that didn't work, but I didn't learn. It was my ego that said yes, I'll do it when Simon offered me another chance. But I will never, ever do an afternoon show again. The trick is to know your limitations. I am not Richard and Judy, I'm not Oprah, I'm not Ellen. I can't do it. Oh well. I definitely had some great opportunities – but I failed. You live and learn.

Of course, everybody wants to succeed and nobody sets out to get bad reviews. At least I was working with amazing people. My producer, Helen Warner, was supportive and we had a great crew – everybody worked their arses off for me. It wasn't their fault the show failed. It was mine.

It was a real lesson learned. I was grateful to Simon for giving me the opportunity, and I felt bad that it hadn't worked out, but at least I knew I wouldn't make that mistake again. *The Vagina Monologues* had reminded me just how much I loved the stage, and soon I was treading the boards again. And this time, Simon was there too.

On 22 November 2006 Elton put on a special charity performance of *Billy Elliot* to mark the millionth person to see the show since it first opened at the Victoria Palace Theatre. This time the charity to benefit was The Place2Be, an organisation of incredibly committed people offering emotional and practical support to children in difficult circumstances in primary schools. The particular school chosen was in Easington in County Durham, just south of Newcastle where much of the original film was shot, which is in an area that was deeply affected by the miners' strike and the pit closures of the early eighties, the period in which the story is set.

When Elton saw the film, he said he could barely watch it he was crying so much. He could see so much of himself in Billy. He told me how it could have been his own childhood and his dream and how he broke out. Working with the original writer Lee Hall, and Stephen Daldry, the original director, he turned it into a musical and, as everyone now knows, an incredible success. I loved it as a film and I loved it as a musical. I must have seen it five or six times before that very special night.

It was special in all sorts of ways. First Liam Mower, the young man who danced Billy in the first cast, came back and did it again for just one night, and Elton himself took a small part, which had everyone up on their feet – it brought the house down. He had only one line, which no one could hear above the clapping and cheering.

There's a scene where Billy has to audition for the Royal Ballet School, and Elton had asked me if I could persuade

# Performance

Simon and Louis to come and, together with me, be the judges on the panel. So we did, and it was so funny and I was thrilled to be a part of it. For the curtain call all three of us put frilly tutus on over our clothes. Louis and I really looked the part, but Simon's face was a picture.

There's something magical about being backstage in a theatre: the smell, pressing yourself into the wall as the cast run past you down the narrow corridors, their beautiful young faces and the over-the-top make-up, the hushed calls over the tannoy, everyone waiting for their cue in the wings, the kids so excited, seeing their profiles half in shadow against the bright glare of the spotlights. I was in my element, and so in awe of the talent of the little Billys and the other boys. I didn't want to leave the theatre, I wanted it to go on for ever, just to be around the atmosphere. I was on such a high that night that when I got home I couldn't sleep. I thought to myself, I would do this every night for free.

# Hollywood

Simon Cowell in a tutu – it still puts a smile on my face more than half a year on.

I had seen Elton again a few weeks ago in Las Vegas, at the Colosseum at Caesar's Palace. He's been doing his Red Piano show since 2004, when it was voted the most exciting show in Vegas. I'd already seen it four times, but I can never see enough of it.

It was Mother's Day – in America it's always the second Sunday in May, not in the early spring as it is in England. He was fabulous, of course, and – as usual – he ended the show with 'Your Song', the song that made him. I have always loved it, but never before have I listened to it with my face streaming with tears. He knew I was in the audience – and he dedicated it to me. Not that anyone in the audience knew. It was in code. One of our games.

'And this is for a very special mother in the audience tonight, the Baroness Dairy Lea.'

We were in Vegas because for once Ozzy's and my schedules crossed. We managed to spend four nights together. Ozzy was being honoured at the VH1 Rock Honors show, the second year MTV's big-sister company had held the event. As the publicity put it: 'The show salutes these groundbreaking bands of rock through spoken tributes, filmed packages and performances by some of today's hottest rock acts, as well as the legends themselves.'

The groundbreaking legends were Ozzy, ZZ Top and Genesis. As well as performing themselves, another band played a cover of a song by the artist being honoured. In Ozzy's case the organisers had suggested Queens of the Stone Age. They were dying to come on, they said; they were huge fans of Ozzy's. I laughed out loud, and said fine. Fine by me.

Queens of the Stone Age are youngish guys who come from Palm Desert in California, and they played Ozzfest in 2000. They played very well but they were a bit too cool for school, thought they were really alternative. In the spring of 2007 the Queens' frontman Josh Homme said in *Blender* magazine that Ozzfest was the worst festival they had ever done, said I'd asked him to go on it this year but he'd said no, because 'they treat the bands like shit. And this year you get to play for free under the guise of, "We're doing it for the fans!" But it's really for the people who fan Sharon and Ozzy with palm fronds at their house.' The magazine asked me to comment, so I did. 'I hope he gets syphilis and dies. I hope his dick fucking falls off.'

So the Queens, as they're called, came on and played Sabbath's 'Paranoid' as their tribute to Ozzy. And it was really well done, note for note like the original. We never spoke to them, they never spoke to us. We did sound checks at different times, our dressing rooms weren't close to each other. Our paths never crossed. It was a good gig for them and for us, and business is business. As far as my curse is concerned, if his trousers are anything to go by, his mother can relax. His manhood is still intact.

Sitting here now with my father, I remember how much he used to love Vegas. He was in his element there. It's only forty-five minutes by plane from Los Angeles, and when my father was in his heyday we'd just go there for the night. It was his way of impressing people. It was like: Let's go to Vegas for the night! We'd charter a Lear jet, see a show and come back. Everyone loved it, especially the bank managers.

We saw the cream of entertainment there, together. Frank Sinatra, Dean Martin, Liberace, Sammy Davis Jnr. It was like the golden age. I saw tham all – all except Elvis, which is a huge, huge regret.

It was always the shows for me, never the gambling. I never gamble. I never win, so I always think, There goes a pair of shoes, a handbag . . . Ozzy is a lucky gambler. He only plays the slot machines but he always wins. And I don't like slot machines.

I don't like the smell of all those coins, but I don't think I'd look quite right wearing white gloves or covering my hands with antiseptic gel.

I was in Las Vegas for a new TV show, one I had never expected to be part of. My father had started out in variety. It's in my blood. And now this new show had brought me full circle. It's funny, isn't it? When my father realised his days as a showman were over, he'd moved into management. He had a great eye for talent, even if he did pass on the Beatles. Gene Vincent, Sabbath, the Small Faces, ELO. Hit after hit. I'd stood right there next to him, and learned so much. And now there I was in Vegas judging a new breed of entertainers, trying to spot fresh talent all over again.

# 7

## America's Got Talent

The morning of 6 April 2007 I woke up feeling extremely sorry for myself. I felt terrible. Although it was good to be back home, my adorable husband was being slightly less than adorable as he was fine-tuning the album *Black Rain*, his ninth studio album and the sixth since 2001's *Down To Earth*. The first track, 'I Don't Wanna Stop', had been released as a teaser single six weeks before. I genuinely thought he was onto a winner, but the music business is fickle and 'sure-fire' doesn't exist. But while I was quietly confident, Ozzy was loudly unconfident, finding every excuse under the sun why the record was sure to fail.

Then Minnie was ill. She'd been off her food and getting thinner and thinner. It sounds stupid to say that you love a dog, but I do love Minnie. Those weeks after my cancer operation when I was hovering somewhere between life and death in bed in Malibu with the sound of the surf crashing outside, and human beings coming and going, whispering quietly, it was Minnie whose steady breathing and warmth seemed to be the only things keeping me from just giving up. They were doing further tests but her heart was enlarged, they said. And she's already eleven. In dog years, an old lady. A very old lady, like me.

*Dancing with the Stars* had been on air since 19 March and I could hardly bear to watch it, though I did. All I could think was that that could have been me up there. Of course, in my imagination I was never the one to be eliminated. I was always among the ones going through to the next round. Ever since the flop of my US chat show, I'd been determined somehow to get back onto US television, and I'd screwed it up. I'd fucked about with my body once too often and now I was paying the price.

I can't now remember what time the call came. I was in the bath and my housekeeper Saba decided I wasn't to be disturbed. Bob, our house manager, had answered the phone. It was Syco. Simon Cowell's office. Could I call him back?

This was it, the call I had been dreading. Just over a month before we'd heard that Louis and Kate were being kicked off *The X-Factor*. Now it was my turn. Call him back? Not fuck-ing likely. He wants to sack me, he can pay for the fucking

*The Sharon Osbourne Show* – faa-bulous! (© Ken McKay/Rex Features)

If I'd known when I invited David Hasselhoff on my show that in less than a year we would be fellow judges on *America's Got Talent*, I'd have asked Minnie to behave more like a lady. (© Ken McKay/Rex Features)

9 October 2006. A triple birthday: mine, my guest Sean Lennon's and his father's – my childhood hero, the late, lamented John Lennon. (© Ken McKay/Rex Features)

Michael Parkinson shows how it's done, by bringing out the best in Lionel Richie, while Liza Minnelli and I look on admiringly. (© Ken McKay/Rex Features)

My suitably attired fellow judges, Simon Cowell (left) and Louis Walsh (right), take a curtain call with Elton and Liam Mower at a gala performance of *Billy Elliot* in November 2006. (© WireImage)

Tony, Saba, Ozzy and me play games for the camera.

*Shrink Rap*: Pamela Stephenson had me in tears. (© WENN)

As a Mother's Day treat I took some of my girlfriends to Elton's Red Piano show at Las Vegas. Elton is the ultimate performer, a true star.

The Queen and I have met on a number of occasions. This was at Buckingham Palace, on 14 February 2007, her annual reception for women 'who have made a significant contribution to business and industry in the United Kingdom'. (© ALPHA Press Agency)

The Ozzfest press conference in February 2007, when Ozzy's announcement of a free Ozzfest was greeted first by silence, then by cheers. (© WENN)

Piers Morgan, David
Hasselhoff and me.
We have had our ups
and downs, but that's
what makes good TV.

Jerry Springer is a true
gentleman.
(© NBCUP/Photobank/Rex Features)

Happy families at the Oscars, 2007. (© ALPHA Press Agency)

Louis Walsh takes over escort duties for the premiere of *Casino Royale*, and we are snapped with David and Elton. (© ALPHA Press Agency)

Gardening at Welders, our house in Buckinghamshire.

call. It wouldn't be a long one. At least, I thought, he had the decency to call me himself. Not like poor Louis. Louis had been in Copenhagen with Shayne Ward when he'd got his call . . . from the director, Richard Holloway. I'll just wait.

I didn't have to wait long to hear Bob's voice on the speaker.

'Simon Cowell for you on line one.'

'Sharon?' said a female voice. 'I've got Simon for you.'

'Hello, sweetheart.' That same old voice with just that hint of a whine. 'How are you?'

'Faa–bulous. Couldn't be better,' I lied.

'Look, I'm not going to beat around the bush, babe. I've got a proposition for you. It's a yes or a no.'

What? Not the sack then? God, I thought. It must be another fucking *Celebrity X-Factor*. What an idiot! It was exactly a year ago that he'd called. It had seemed a gift at the time. A week having a bit of a laugh for charity, and being paid for it . . .

This time I would say no. Or, at the very least, I'd insist on finding out who the contestants were, though it's hard to imagine they could scrape further down the barrel of awfulness.

'Go on then. I'm listening.'

'*America's Got Talent*.'

What? 'What do you mean, Simon?'

'*America's Got Talent*. It's a show I do . . . similar thing to *The X*—'

'I know what it is, you idiot . . .' It had been one of Ozzy's

167

and my favourite shows in its first season. Hilarious and a huge success. 'What about it?'

'Well, because of what's happened with Brandy, there's a vacancy on the panel.'

Brandy, the sole female judge, had been involved in a tragic road accident the previous Christmas.

'You mean . . . to replace Brandy . . . you want . . . ?'

'Yeah. Look, I know it's short notice – auditions start in a couple of weeks – but financially I don't think we're going to be fighting too hard.'

Reader, I said yes.

The first series of *America's Got Talent* was NBC's top show. I saw no reason why the second series would be any different.

Simon Cowell is one of the great TV innovators. Nor does he just sit back and get others to do the work. Simon's out there at the rock face on *The X-Factor*, day after day, week after week. He doesn't have to do it, but he knows that Mr Nasty is central to the show's success, and that it wouldn't be the same without him. It's the S-Factor.

*America's Got Talent* is yet another of Simon's genius ideas. It's all a question of timing, and he has this knack of judging the public's appetite. It's nothing new. Anyone of the generation that remembers *Opportunity Knocks* will recognise the format. Variety artists came on, were interviewed by Hughie

Greene, then the public voted for their favourites, by post in those days, of course. There was another programme called *New Faces*, but that one had a panel of experts. *Opportunity Knocks* was the first one that let the public decide.

The format is now incredibly familiar, from *Pop Idol* onwards, but it took Simon to realise that not everybody can sing (and that includes most of *The X-Factor* hopefuls), and that there's a whole lot of different talents out there, which, at the moment, have nowhere to go.

Ever since television arrived, people have been saying that variety is dead. Before then variety – or vaudeville as it's called in America – was everywhere. Singers were just one act in a bill that could include acrobats, jugglers, comedians, magicians, dog acts, high-wire acts, clowns, dancers, animal noises. Anything. Absolutely anything as long as it made you laugh, made you gasp, kept you enthralled, as long as it entertained.

And, of course, the extraordinary thing is that variety is in my blood. So far from being a we-can't-have-Brandy-so-we're-stuck-with-Sharon compromise, it's tailor-made for me. Plus for me it's total luxury: you turn up, there's no script, no mentoring involved, you say what you think and you fuck off home.

Yes, I knew Simon had the show, but it had never occurred to me for one moment that I'd be on his list. Why? Because I was Mrs X-Factor. Plus I'd fucked up on his chat show. And taking me out of my natural home would not be a good idea – that's how he would look at it. I already knew that an

English version was in the pipeline – and he hadn't wanted me for that.

Top prize for the *Britain's Got Talent* was a spot on the Royal Variety Show. Coincidentally, I had co-hosted the Royal Variety Show with Michael Parkinson the year before. I'd had a great time. As a kid I lived and breathed variety. I was born in Brixton, where a lot of variety artists were based, and I was brought up among them. In that world, the Royal Variety Show was the pinnacle everybody aspired to. I don't know how many times I must have watched it on TV over the years. All the great stars of the day would come on, and it was often the only time you ever saw them. So for me it was just a fantastic thing to be a part of. Ozzy performed 'In My Life', and Dame Shirley Bassey headlined. Not everyone appreciated it, though. When the Queen and Prince Philip came backstage to meet the artists, as they do at every command performance, I said to the Prince: 'So, did you enjoy the show then, sir?'

'What do you think?' he said.

The expression on his face gave me the answer. 'No,' I said.

'You're right. It was too loud and too long and I didn't understand any of it.'

Miserable old bastard.

There's no equivalent of the Royal Variety Show in America. There it's just cash. I say 'just', though no one's going to sniff at a million dollars. And in America there is already much more scope for variety acts than there is in

Britain. Las Vegas is variety central. Every single hotel has a show and Las Vegas is Las Vegas: the costumes, the acts, the sets, everything is completely over the top. There are great possibilities out there because for so long there's been stagnation. Come up with something different, and the sky's the limit as far as career possibilities go. There's a whole new generation of entertainers who are looking to take their skills to a whole new level of sophistication: ventriloquists, magicians, illusionists.

Brandy wasn't the only change in the line-up. The host for the first series had been Regis Philbin, a very well-known American presenter. But Regis had only recently got over a heart attack, so for the second series Jerry Springer took over.

Jerry Springer – as they often say on TV – needs no introduction, except that most people don't know that he's actually a Londoner, born in East Finchley tube station of all places – his parents were Jewish refugees. Which meant that of the four regulars on *America's Got Talent*, only one was born in the USA – David Hasselhoff.

What can you say about the Hoff, as he is called by everyone? He's larger than life – literally; he towers over me – and completely unpredictable. In Britain he is probably best known for *Knight Rider*, the hit show from the eighties, and of course *Baywatch*. It was through his determination that *Baywatch* became such a huge success. The first series was written off as a dud, but the Hoff bought the rights and then, acting in it and producing, it went on to run for years and years to make it the most globally successful TV series ever. To say that he doesn't need to work is putting it mildly, and yet he does. First and last he's an entertainer. Quite mad, but such fun to be with as he's permanently sending himself up. During the audition period of the show, he was still performing in Vegas in the musical of *The Producers*, where he was playing the camp director of the spoof Nazi musical, *Springtime for Hitler*. He is also of course a very successful singer (erm, erm . . .). However you look at it, a judge with every possible credential.

Which brings me nicely to the third member of the panel, and the third Brit in the line-up: Piers Morgan, whose credentials to judge a variety competition would frankly appear to be zero, beyond the fact that he was once editor of the *Daily Mirror*. Now, just as I said that Chris Tarrant and I had no baggage, beyond his inability to be civil, the same is not true of the Osbournes and Piers Morgan. When I said yes to Simon I had temporarily forgotten who the other panellist was. I was just so happy to be doing it.

The first time I met Piers was that occasion in March 2004 when Chris Tarrant studiously avoided even saying hello to Ozzy and me at the Pride of Britain Awards. Piers, on the contrary, was very polite in a legless kind of way. He was red-faced, red-nosed, loud-mouthed, very confident. And what else would you expect from a British tabloid editor? The *Mirror* is hardly the *Financial Times* or the *Wall Street Journal*.

172

The next time we crossed paths was in the summer of 2006. We were in Los Angeles, and my publicist Gary called. He said that Piers Morgan wanted to film an interview with Ozzy for the BBC. It was like a biography piece. So I thought, that'll be nice, a little biography piece on Ozzy's career. Yes, Gary, I said. Tell him we'll do the show.

So Piers flies out, and they get a local production crew and come to the house in Doheny Road. And Ozzy gives him a tour of the premises and the rest of it and then they do the interview. They whip through the early years of Sabbath, but then it seems to come to a full stop. Nothing about the amazing career he's had for the last quarter-century. Piers just kept harping on about when Ozzy was fired by the band.

'So what actually happened?' he asked yet again.

'I really don't know what went down,' said Ozzy. 'I was just told to fuck off.'

'So what effect did that have on you?' said Piers.

'Well, the rest of the day was pretty fucked.'

And this went on and on. About groupies and drugs, the drinking, about being kicked out of Sabbath. It was insane. Piers kept going back over the old ground again and again. And Ozzy kept saying, 'Can we move on now?'

'Look, Piers,' he said finally, 'just tell me what you want me to say and I'll fucking say it! Anything to get this thing over with.' He said afterwards it was like being interrogated by the fucking Gestapo.

It was several days later when we discovered what had been going on. This wasn't a profile of Ozzy, it was a series called *You Can't Fire Me, I'm Famous*. I was furious. I felt that the production company had got Ozzy under false pretences. They'd sold it to us as a biography piece. If they'd told us what it was about – famous people who'd been fired – then fine. You do it or you don't. But don't entice somebody to do something by lying. I mean, what were they doing, buttering up Ozzy's ego by saying it was an hour's piece on his life? It's so cheap. Typical tabloid, typical Piers.

We'd filmed it, the contract had been signed but there was one thing they hadn't covered. Clearance. We hadn't signed the clearance form. From then on we had complete control. If they didn't want to just chuck it in the bin, we'd edit it the way we wanted. And we did. The stupid thing is that Ozzy wasn't ashamed of being fired from Sabbath. Quite the opposite. It was the best thing that had ever happened to him. It wasn't like he was the editor of a national newspaper who got publicly humiliated and fired.

What really stuck in my throat was just the way they went about it: it was underhand and slimy. Piers knew what was going on. It was his show, for fuck's sake. He could have told the truth and we would probably have done it anyway. I didn't dislike him. I liked him. I knew what he was, but I liked him anyway. He definitely has charm.

Piers had interviewed me too, at the Groucho Club in London in June 2005, more or less exactly a year before the business with Ozzy's interview. It was for *GQ*, a classy men's magazine. Well, as classy as any men's mag gets. We had a gas. A real gas. Because I know what he's like, I got Gary to arrange to see the interview before it was published. It's called copy approval. We took out a couple of things, scurrilous things I thought wouldn't go down well in certain camps, and that was that. He didn't have the right to sell it to any other newspaper; it was *GQ* or nothing.

Or so I thought. Just a couple of weeks before I got the call from Simon, Gary called me from London. The *Daily Mail* were running extracts of Piers's latest book of gossip, he said: chats with the famous, and our jolly lunch was in it. All of it. Not the edited highlights that had appeared in *GQ* but the full shebang.

And so it was. Everything. What I'd paid for my surgery, how much my face cost, how much my tits cost. How I think Melanie Griffiths has destroyed her looks with a terrible face job, and Mickey Rourke and Michael Douglas for that matter. What I said about Bono, Madonna, Brian Ferry, Mick Jagger. Basically I said they were the most boring stuck-up celebs you could ever meet, and I think I called them cunts or whatever. I'm sure it's going to change their lives as much as it's gonna change mine. Who gives a shit? Everything he said I said, I did say. And when you say things, you have to take responsibility. And I do. But it was all 'off the record', as they put it in journalistic circles. It's like a gentleman's agreement that you don't use it. It was simply the fact that he could have called and warned me. He could have said, Listen, Sharon. The stuff you said off the record, I'm going to use it in my book. Just going to pre-warn you. But no.

So the day before the first day of filming, NBC arranged a little getting-to-know-you dinner. I was very much the new girl. I hadn't worked with any of them before: not Piers, not Jerry, not the Hoff, not even NBC. So I put on my most fabulous outfit and a car came to pick me up and took me to Mr Chow's. It's been there since the seventies and is a favourite place of mine; one street west of Rodeo Drive, très chic with its black-and-white floor and A-list clientele. It's as far removed from the Chinese restaurants of my childhood as it's possible to imagine. One way and another I should have been feeling very up. But I wasn't.

Earlier in the day, there'd been a call from Gary in London.

'So you're having dinner with Piers Morgan tonight, I gather.'

'Where did you get that from?'

'Oh, it's in the *Mail*. Piers mentioned it in his column. And about how you're really pissed off with him.'

So, I thought, the little shit is still at it. OK. I just have to accept that from now on nothing is confidential. Not that it's any big deal, but it's like, for fuck's sake. Is nothing sacred with him? And then I remembered a rather good phrase he'd come up with, talking about himself. 'One day you're cock of the walk and the next you're a feather duster.' Couldn't have put it better myself.

The dinner was in a private room right at the top of the building and, of course, as always, I was the last to arrive. We all get introduced: a young English producer on the show, James Sunderland, who Simon had brought over from *The X-Factor* and who I first worked with on the Royal Variety Performance; then there were a couple of heads from the production company and NBC, Piers and Jerry Springer. David Hasselhoff wasn't there. I had never met Jerry before, and so they had left the chair for me next to him.

That was the first surprise of the evening. Jerry Springer is a really gracious man. He's highly intelligent. Started out life as a lawyer, and was a political campaign aide to Robert Kennedy. Later he ran for Congress, but didn't make it. He eventually became mayor of Cincinnati and only gave up politics when his broadcasting career took off. *The Jerry Springer Show* was originally serious and issue-driven; it only became the terrible screaming match it turned into later, thanks to that scourge of American TV, the ratings. I found it hard to believe that this gentle, humorous man beside me could be involved with any of that.

While Jerry and I were getting to know each other, Piers was holding forth at the top of the table, generally hogging the conversation and, as far as I could see, it was all me, me, me. It was only when we'd finished our starters – about an hour after I arrived – that the conversation turned to include Mrs Osbourne.

'I trust,' said Piers, 'that you've forgiven me now.'

I smiled sweetly and said nothing.

'Don't think,' he said, 'that you're going to be able to manipulate me the way you manipulate everyone else in your life. I'm not a pushover.'

Well, that was it. I'd been holding all this stuff in, behaving myself, not saying anything and I lost it. I exploded.

'You pen-pushing little twat, you bottom feeder! You're just the scum of the press, you've been fired from every job you've ever had. You are so desperate to be famous it's just pathetic.'

'Now hold on here, Sharon. This isn't exactly professional behaviour, is it?'

'Don't you start on me. Don't you dare call me unprofessional. You're just a fucking middle-class pillock from England.'

'Save it for someone who gives a shit, Sharon.'

'Who do you think you are, talking to me like that? I don't manipulate everyone in my life. You know nothing about me, you don't know me well enough to say that about me.'

The rest of them were sitting there, mouths open. I pushed back my chair, heard something go with a crash – a glass probably – and I walked over to the top of the table. I detested him at this point. I wanted to slap his face and to spit at him. I wanted to hurt him, to physically hurt him. But I didn't. I stood over him and just kept pushing him, tapping at his pudgy pudding face.

'Wake up, darling,' I said. 'You're not Simon Cowell. You're not a visionary. You're just one lucky sonofabitch that got a gig. And it worked for you. But you're not Simon Cowell and you never will be. I've seen you. You haven't got the pedigree to be Mr Mean.'

'Get your hands off me,' he snarled. 'And don't you EVER touch me again!'

By this time two of the NBC guys have got out of their chairs and are standing behind me, trying to drag me out of there.

'I'm going,' I said, looking at him. 'But you just wait, kid. Don't think it's over. This is just the beginning of what I've got in store for you.' I was like a volcano, wanting to spit and explode with all this anger, to get it out of me.

At some point Jerry had tried to intervene but by now had given up and left. Eventually the two NBC guys escorted me out of the restaurant. Down two flights and into the car. The driver was there waiting. I got in, the car pulled away and I called Silvana.

'Oh my God, Silvana. You'll never believe what just happened. Puss has been a bit naughty.' Because by then I felt comparatively normal. All the anger had gone. 'I pretty near slapped the fucker. Look, I'm on my way home. Could you call James and have him call me at Doheny? I'll be there in five.'

James was the young English producer who I was already feeling really bad about.

A couple of minutes later she called me back.

'So what's his version?'

'Pretty much the same as yours. I told him that I thought it would be OK. I explained that you had a beef with Piers and that you're both professional enough to move on. To be honest, Sharon, I think it's better that you did this now. Got it out of the way at the very beginning. I mean, it's a shame, but you know what? Hopefully the two of you can get on.'

'Thanks, Silvany.'

Ozzy knew the moment I arrived at the bedroom door. He said it took me longer to get dressed than it took me to get back.

'So what happened?' he said.

I burst into tears. 'That Piers Morgan. I hate him. He's horrid. He's just a pig.'

Holding me and rocking me gently, Ozzy let me cry.

'Just let it out, let it all out,' he murmured.

There was no way I could leave now. The contract was signed and, let me tell you something, you do not fuck with those networks in America. They are like the old movie studios where they sign you up and they have you, lock, stock and barrel. The only way out is when they fire you, and that's their call, not yours.

'Remember one thing, Sharon. You're a pro and he's not. If I were you I'd just call him up and say, "You know what I think of you, we're never going to be friends, but we have to work together so let's move on."'

So I did. He was at the Wilshire Hotel and he now claims that we spoke for about forty minutes, but he can't remember what we said, and neither can I. He'd left the restaurant straight after me and had taken a sleeping pill.

Next I called Jerry and apologised for my behaviour. I really didn't want him to think badly of me. I told him that I wasn't really a nutcase but that it had been building up inside me. He just laughed. Didn't say a word in condemnation. Not against me, not against Piers. Nothing. He should have been a diplomat. All he said at the end was, OK, see you tomorrow on the set.

The set was CBS Studios in Sherman Oaks in the Valley. So, first day at a new job and I'm a wreck. Thank God the Hoff was there to act as a buffer. He hadn't been there the night before, but he had been a guest on my London talk show and Minnie had attacked him because of the bits of chicken on the seat. The sofa was ivory-coloured so he had no idea he was sitting on a cushion of chicken, and Minnie went straight for his crotch because she could smell the meat. When he tried to move her, she attacked him. He still doesn't know why, though fortunately he doesn't hold it against me.

I couldn't say the same about Piers. The atmosphere was dreadful. Just awful. I wouldn't give him eye contact and he was just snarling at me. It was not a good start.

That first day would have been difficult even without the added entertainment of the night before. I was the new girl coming in to something that was already established. Everybody knew each other, everybody had their own little in-jokes. I know how it is. As for Piers, he really knew how to rile me. He's the kind of person who, whatever you say, he'll just agree. You could call him an ignorant orang-utan and he'd say, 'Yes, you're absolutely right', which of course makes you want to shake him even more. You could feel the tension in the room.

First off, we had a meeting where a couple of the producers talked us through the show and what was going to happen that day. I'd watched the first season so I knew roughly how it all worked.

The studio is a classic movie sound stage, a big box with something vaguely like a theatre built inside it. There's a backstage area and wings, and the audience are in front with the judges sitting among them. Unlike *The X-Factor* there's an audience all through the audition period. To set the scene, they film you backstage, ask the usual kind of questions: What are you expecting today, etc. And when the cameras were rolling I noticed that Piers was like a moth to a flame, and I realised something: that he was a rookie. He was like a kid who'd won a competition and this was the prize. And I suddenly felt: Ah, bless.

Then the auditions start and these acts come out and do whatever they do. For once that phrase 'from the sublime to the ridiculous' is totally the case. Anyway, although the atmosphere was dire, we survived.

That was day one. But something was always going to blow, and it happened about three days in.

I began to notice that Piers was being overcritical with the younger people on the show. There is no age limit on *America's Got Talent* – we had seven-year-olds, even five-year-olds – and I was soon feeling uncomfortable. He was treating these kids as if they could handle rejection, and I thought this was insane behaviour. It's like, Whoa, just a minute here! It seemed to me that he was just showing how clever he is. Doing his Mr Mean impersonation. And I'm thinking to myself: I don't like him anyway, he's making me uncomfortable, he's being mean to the kids.

There was this nine-year-old cheerleader with little blonde plaits, and she wasn't very good, and Piers laid into her. He said she'd been put up to it because her mother wanted her to win a million dollars. And this little thing says no, that she was doing it because she wanted to. It was just horrific. So I thought: Bollocks to this, I'm going to fire myself, before anyone else does. I'm leaving.

And that's what I did. I said, 'I didn't sign up for this. I will not be a party to this', and ripped up all my papers, threw them at him and walked off the set back down the corridor to my dressing room, ripping off my false eyelashes as I went, still shouting, 'I didn't sign up for this.'

Silvana locked the door behind me to stop anyone else coming in. Minutes later I heard Piers ranting down the corridor, saying what did I think I was playing at, and that I was behaving like a fourteen-year-old.

It wasn't put on. I wasn't playing games. I genuinely

wanted out. Jude and Silvana and Saba were there; Saba, my housekeeper, who also acts as my dresser when I'm in LA. Silvana and Saba were both very quiet but Jude didn't have any such qualms – he was rolling his eyes and tearing out his hair.

'Oh my God, Sha-rone! You can't leave . . . I've just cancelled all my work for the next month!'

I called Ozzy and told him what had happened.

'You can't do that, Shaz, because then he's won. He wants you to leave, don't you see?'

And he was right. Ozzy has laser instincts. I could not let Piers bloody Morgan think he'd forced me into walking. In the meantime, I just sat and moped and stroked the dogs, waiting for the knock at the door.

I wondered how they would word it: 'Considering the bumpy start, perhaps it's better that you do go . . .' They were definitely going to do it. I said to myself: What am I doing here? I mean, have a go at an adult who knows what they're doing, by all means, but not a child, who – and in this Piers was right – was probably only here because her parents had pushed her. I'm not doing it any more. I've got to go home and live with myself.

After about forty minutes somebody knocks at the door. I recognise James's gentle English voice. Silvana talks to him.

'How long does she need before she goes back to the set?'

So I went back. The little girl didn't get through and that

was the right decision, but there's a way of letting people down nicely.

*America's Got Talent* was the number-one show that week, and the biggest audience figures NBC have had since January. So I guess something was working between us all.

I began to realise that Piers' behaviour towards me was probably all because he felt threatened. He gets on well with everybody at NBC, he's a professional and this was his stomping ground. Piers loves to be the centre of attention – he doesn't take well to being a bit player, he has to be the star and he likes to hold court. And I think that he loves being in America where he's terribly British and knows about everything – Piers can always join in the conversation because he's very well educated and opinionated. I'm sure he was a prefect at school and told on everyone.

I don't think he liked the fact that it was me that came in. Brandy was a young kid, and he could walk all over her. But after a while the situation between us quietened down. He writes a blog for the *Daily Mail*, and he had actually been quite complimentary about me: 'She's opinionated, fiery and unpredictable. But I have to admit she's also fantastic fun to work with, and knows what she's talking about.'

Also we'd lived through the trauma of the Hoff's terrible exposure on television the week before. One of David Hasselhoff's kids had taken a video of him horribly drunk, lying on the floor, and trying – and failing – to eat a hamburger. When he'd been sober a few days earlier, he'd asked her to film him if ever he got drunk again. He wanted to know what he looked like. Then somebody gave it to the press.

Of course I watched it, like everybody else across America. It was humiliating and I felt sad for him. We all did. We have all been there. We have all been drunk. He wasn't violent. He didn't hurt anybody. When his daughter asked him on film why he drank, he answered, 'Because I'm lonely.' For anybody to have given that film to the press is an action that deserves only contempt. All it did was underline the fact that David has a drink problem and that he needs help. Just like millions of other people. And that's nothing to be ashamed of.

We spent two and a half days filming the 'boot camp' section of the show in Vegas, and they were marked by a bizarre accident. There was an act called Ivan the Urban Action Man, who was a street-style tumbler and acrobat. The idea was that he would spring off a trampoline over a line of stacking chairs – about nine of them were lined up. For safety reasons he wasn't allowed to bring in his own trampoline, so he used one provided by Production. But just as he jumped on this bloody thing, it broke, and instead of leaping over the chairs he went crashing into them.

At first I thought it was part of the stunt, as we all did. He just lay there, arms by his sides, flat like a toy soldier that had been knocked over. In the boot camp there is no audience as such, but the other acts are allowed to watch and they sit behind the judges. First there was a general murmuring behind me, then deathly silence.

Jerry was looking more worried than I had ever seen him, and it was only then that I was convinced this was for real.

'I don't know what's more nerve-racking, being a judge or being up here,' he said to camera. 'This was not supposed to happen. The question is whether he landed on his head. This was not part of the act. He's lying still. This is a horrible moment. He's not responding.' And he wasn't. By this time a curtain had been pulled across so that the audience – the other contestants – didn't see. I walked behind with Silvana to see what was going on.

He was out cold for several minutes – motionless, totally still – but then he sprang to his feet, and I have never seen anyone get up so quick. He looked at us all, like, What gives? I knew from what happened with Ozzy's accident that when you're in shock adrenalin kicks in, so I was worried. He was walking, but unsteadily – just like Ozzy did. I knew the walking meant nothing. He could have broken his neck. They took it seriously, had him taken straight to hospital and later we found out there was no permanent damage; he had just knocked himself out. Then they told us he wouldn't be coming back. There's no business like show business.

In the end Piers and I worked together just fine. I think he has tried to model himself on Simon with his Mr Mean act, but they're very different. Simon is an entrepreneur. Simon is Barnum & Bailey. He has great comic timing, which people don't always give him credit for. His one-liners are incredible.

He's multi-talented. One minute he's a judge, the next minute he's in the editing suite.

As for Piers, to be honest I think he's wasted being a judge. Like him or hate him, he definitely does have a presence about him. He's excellent on TV. I think he could be the new Larry King – whoops, I can't believe I just wrote that about him.

# Hollywood

I wonder how long I've been sitting here? It's hard to tell. Time seems to slow down when you're with someone who can't respond. It can't be so long. The music is still playing quietly in the background.

It's a luxury to have some quiet time today. I've been working on two huge shows at the same time on two different continents. Not only *America's Got Talent*, but also *The X-Factor*.

Behind the scenes, the final shows of the third season were to prove dramatic for me. And it all stemmed from this room where I'm now sitting.

About three weeks before Christmas 2006 I'd had a phone call from the Belmont. A cold had led to pneumonia, they said, and my father had been taken into Cedars-Sinai. I called the hospital immediately. They know me well, it's one of the largest private hospitals in the world and it's where I had my cancer treated – and everything else for that matter. If you could buy a season ticket, I should get one.

The doctors said that it really didn't look good. 'The most he has left to live is a couple of weeks.'

The call came at around four in the morning. I was back in England, at Welders. Ozzy was still asleep – the phone hadn't woken him because the television was still on. I got out of bed and went downstairs to the kitchen to make myself a cup of tea and to think. Minnie came with me. The doctors had asked me what I wanted to do and I said I didn't know, and I didn't. The fire was still just about alight. I put another log on it and watched the flames flare up. Beau gave a stretch and then went back to sleep again. Sonny didn't move. He's fifteen now, handsome as ever but as deaf as a post. I'm amazed he's still alive.

The X-Factor still had a couple of weeks to run. A twenty-four-hour in-and-out turnaround to LA might just be possible, but what would be the point? My relationship with my father was, to say the least, ambivalent. On many levels he had been a monster. Certainly that was how the world saw him. But he was my father and I was my father's daughter. All those years, no matter what he did to me, I never stopped loving him.

My father had no future and no past. As for the present, it was simply distressing for him. Any change to the routine and

he was terrified. The hospital told me that he was being unco-
operative. He didn't understand that he had to stay in bed. He
was constantly trying to move, and like many Alzheimer sufferers, would sometimes get aggressive. In the end they had to
restrain him, tie him down in his cot. He was obviously panicked
and frightened. In a strange environment surrounded by new
faces. How much he understood of what was going on, I have
no idea.

Sitting on the sofa at Welders with my feet curled up under
me, Minnie by my side, her nose on my lap, I thought about
what the doctors had said.

'We need to know what you want to do with your father. We
need to make arrangements.'

I didn't understand.

'Do you want him to be resuscitated?' they asked.

Pneumonia used to be known as the old man's friend,
because it took you out. Finally I understood that it was a question of medication, and I asked them what would happen if the
pneumonia was allowed to go its natural course, with no outside
intervention. They had said – in layman's language – that his
lungs would fill with water and he would drown. It was my
father. My money paying for the hospital. My call.

Do you want him to be resuscitated . . .

You think it's so simple: no need to prolong a life that isn't a
life any more. I'd always imagined I would be strong and that I'd
make the decision. But when somebody says to you, 'What do
you want to do?' – it's a whole different thing. I felt fear.

If there was a point where he'd gone and he had to be revived, or he was on a life-support system, then I'd say, Just turn it off, but I knew I couldn't be responsible for not giving him medication.

Perhaps there's a part of me that fears what people might think, because even though I never stopped loving him, there were times when I definitely felt hatred. Perhaps I feared that people might think that finally I was taking my revenge now that I had the upper hand.

I felt sick with fear. The idea that if he died because I'd denied him medication was abhorrent to me. That I'd had the power to save him but didn't. I couldn't be responsible for that. I couldn't let him drown. My mind came up with all these images and it was horrible. Just horrible. I couldn't be responsible for that. In theory it sounded simple – something I had taken for granted for years and years. Faced with the reality it terrified me. It was a huge learning experience for me.

That was when Aimee stepped in. I called her the next morning and told her about my dilemma – that I couldn't make up my mind. She stopped me in mid-sentence. 'Mum,' she said. 'Let me go and see him. You need someone to go and visit, just to see what kind of shape he's in. I'm here, I can do that for you.'

I was so moved. My wonderful daughter, who had decided not to meet her grandfather because she didn't want to experience the pain of losing him – was prepared to go now just to help me. So she went, and I was so grateful.

In the end I called them up and told them I couldn't do it. 'You have to give him whatever you can to save him.'

So they gave him an intravenous antibiotic, and he pulled through.

Why did I do it? It's not as if he had any quality of life. He didn't. Physically the pneumonia took its toll on his poor old body and he ended up worse than he was before. After his fall at Christmas, he was confined to a wheelchair. He couldn't walk, he couldn't even sit up without assistance. He couldn't feed himself, couldn't do anything for himself any more. He just lay there.

Then, just a few weeks later, he began to vomit and clutch his stomach. Dari, who was there at his side every step of the way, sent for an ambulance and he went to Cedars-Sinai hospital, yet again. There they put him on a glucose drip. Again he was tied to a cot so he wouldn't fall. After a couple of days the pain seemed to subside, so he was allowed back to Belmont.

After his release from Cedars they had told me, yet again, that they couldn't see him surviving more than a couple of weeks, the same thing they had told me with the pneumonia six months earlier. I agonised over what I had done, over what I should do if the situation should arise again. He must be so tired, I thought, and in so much inner pain. Talking to Dari, who had cared for him with such dignity for nearly two years, I said, 'I think he's had it, he's had enough.'

Why didn't I let the pneumonia take him at Cedars-Sinai? He

would have been in good company: Lucille Ball, Sammy Kahn, Sammy Davis Jnr, Danny Kaye, they all breathed their last at Cedars-Sinai. Even his great hero, Frank Sinatra. Perhaps the ultimate revenge is keeping him alive, in one of these places that Ozzy calls God's waiting room.

I'm terrified that the same thing – the dementia – is going to happen to me. Alzheimer's is such a cruel death. It's horrific. Worse than any cancer. It's the cruellest death of all.

If this disease is to be my fate, I don't want to repeat history and go through what my father has gone through. I just wouldn't want my loved ones to see me this way. I've discussed it with my family and we have a plan in place. My kids would take me to Switzerland where euthanasia is legal, and you can die with dignity.

I want to go while I still have control – me being the ultimate control freak. And what an unbelievable chance to put your life in order and choose your point of departure.

I don't want to be a burden to the people I love.

# 8

## *The X-Factor*

'*N*on, rien de rien. Non, je ne regrette rien.' Let the madness begin. *X-Factor* auditions, series four.

I can't stop singing it. The song the great French singer Edith Piaf made famous. This woman was the best thing we had this morning. I told Simon I thought she was multi-talented. And she was. She said she could play four invisible instruments. She made musical-instrument noises with her nose and mouth and could sing in ten different languages. And she did rap. All at the age of eighty.

How good is it to have Louis back? No matter how crazy it gets we can always have a laugh to break up the tension. As I said on camera a few minutes ago – footage for the official welcome back: 'It's like having your mate back at school. You know when you change schools and miss your best friend? It's as if they suddenly come back.'

I know how that feels because it happened to me with my best friend Posy when I was about twelve. I was made to leave my first stage school, Italia Conti, because my brother and I weren't getting on. He being the oldest, I was the one that had to leave. I was sent to Ada Foster's, another stage school miles away on the other side of London. Posy missed me as much as I missed her and amazingly her parents let her join me. She was my first proper friend. It was seeing her with her family that showed me life didn't have to be about guns and violence and shouting all the time.

When I heard on the news in March this year that Louis had been sacked, I did not believe it. The press must have got it wrong, I decided. I would have heard, got some whisper of it anyway. If they said I'd been sacked I'd have been less surprised. According to the press, Mrs O was always heading for the chop as I had the habit of getting up Simon's nose and generally behaving badly.

When I found out it was true, that Louis really had been let go, I was devastated. The only way you can commit yourself to six months on a show like this is if it's fun. And it had been. Each of the three series, thanks to Louis. And there I was signed, sealed and delivered up for a fourth series and my best friend had gone. I talked to Ozzy about it and decided it was best not to get involved. It's Simon's show, he created it, it's his baby. You're just employed to do a job, not to make decisions.

Now that Louis is well and truly back, the word in the press is that the whole sacking business was a put-up job, a PR stunt to ratchet up publicity for the show. Not true. It was a moment of total aberration on the part of Simon and ITV. They broke the cardinal rule of business success: if it ain't broke, don't fix it. For three years now *The X-Factor* had owned Saturday nights. What the fuck were they thinking of, changing anything at all? We were the ideal panel: sweet-natured Louis was the ultimate foil for Simon's lacerating tongue. Plus he knew his stuff. They were the perfect double-act with me as Aunt Sally in the middle.

What made it work so well between the three of us is that we're all so different, yet each of us has a great deal of experience in our own area of music. We've all been successful on the business side and know what we're talking about, but in different genres. And we're a real mix in terms of our personalities, and that made it interesting. Individually, our tastes are so varied. Louis would see something, spot some talent in someone, and I was like, 'Are you nuts?' It was the same for all of us.

That's what makes a good panel – you have to have a good mix. It doesn't work if you all like the same thing. It would be boring if we all agreed with Simon.

Before Louis returned we continued our relationship as usual. We still socialised and spoke regularly. I invited him on as my guest on *The Friday Night Project*, a comedy show on ITV where they get a different celebrity to host each episode, ask their own guests and then create havoc. Among other sur-real sketches, I persuaded him to dress up as Amy Winehouse. Ozzy, who was my other guest, said Louis looked more like Amy Winehouse than Amy Winehouse did. We had a great time, trying to make light of the fact that I was back on *The X-Factor* and he wasn't, and slagging off Simon like a pair or old tarts sounding off about their pimp. Louis confessed he was missing everyone dreadfully. Well, if it's any consolation, I said, everyone is missing you. And we were.

The first day of auditions in London without him was unbe-lievably bad, and I was in a horrible mood. It just wasn't the same without Louis and I wasn't going to pretend that it was. There was nothing wrong with Brian Friedman, who I am sure is a perfectly nice man. He is certainly a good choreo-grapher and the programme could do with that. As for Dannii Minogue, she is far from the flossy airhead I thought she would be. She might look like the most perfect porcelain doll, but she is sharp and feisty and nobody's fool. She's very ambitious and she knows what she wants. We're from a different generation, but I respect her and she brings a new dynamic to the show.

But that first day I made no effort to go out of my way for them. I was a hair's breadth short of hostile. You're big people, I thought, you find your own comfort level. I know I behaved badly, calling Brian the Rude American, which the contest-ants picked up on. They then said to him, 'Go back to your own country, get on back to where you belong.' I was defi-nitely winding everybody up.

Alan Carr and Justin Lee Collins help me out at London Zoo for *The Friday Night Project*. (© PA Photos)

Justin Lee Collins and Alan Carr play Kelly and Ozzy in an *Osbournes'* spoof for *The Friday Night Project*. (© PA Photos)

Louis, me and Simon are rendered speechless (in wax) at Madame Tussauds.
(© ALPHA Press Agency)

*The X-Factor* boot camp, 2007. When it all gets too much, Louis and I can always have a laugh together.

Patricia O'Neill has been doing my make-up and hair since the first series of *The X-Factor*.

Sharon Osbourne, tourist. St Isaac's Cathedral in St Petersburg.

Saba packing up our bedroom at Doheny. It took fifteen men working ten days to clear the house.

Sharing a joke with Minnie at Malibu.

Just returned from taking Mr Chips for a walk on the beach at Malibu.

Within days of taking possession of the house at Hidden Hills, the curse of the Osbournes struck again when the pool mysteriously caved in.

Two blondes, each better known
for having hair another colour.
(© Brian Aris)

Jackie Boy putting up with
maternal affection in public
(my chat show).

Dromoland Castle, Co. Clare, Ireland. Romantic setting for our twenty-fifth wedding anniversary.

Twenty-five years and more in love than ever. (© Brian Aris)

By the fountains in the garden at Welders. (© Brian Aris)

Dermot O'Leary, the new presenter, I took too straight away. I'd never met him before but the kids knew him. He's a great bloke, very grounded, with a big heart. He says he feels he needs to go and have therapy sessions because he gets so involved and pulled into everyone's story.

The London auditions were held at Arsenal's brand new football stadium, which was still smelling of new carpet and new paint. The green room had all the charm of a departure lounge. I constantly expected to be told to go to Gate 21 where my flight was ready to take off. When I wasn't needed on set, I preferred to go to my dressing room (one of the corporate boxes looking down onto the pitch) and talk with my make-up artist Trisha about the good ol' days of the first series when there was no money. The studio was in Wembley then, and we were there right up to the time it was demolished. There would always be the smell of damp with a hint of the sewer about it – you felt that if you didn't keep moving, you'd end up covered in mould. It was horrible, dirty and old, yet that first week, in the swanky new Arsenal stadium, I wished we were back in that gloomy, smelly old building. It was a new show with a small budget and everyone chipped in more. There were no private planes – we travelled by train and stayed at pretty crap hotels. But I liked all that – there's nothing that can take away the excitement of something new. I've seen it so many times before in my years on the road with Ozzy, and even before. You think that by piling more money into the production you'll make it better. But sometimes in doing so you lose the thing you had. But hey! What do I know?

So here we are in Manchester, and I can see Louis out of the corner of my eye, trying not to giggle. He's a terrible giggler, can't help himself.

This is my fourth year of doing *The X-Factor* and you'd think I'd be used to it by now, but I never cease to be amazed at the people who genuinely think they can sing and haven't the slightest idea that they can't.

Naturally, we all egg them on, asking complete no-hopers if they think they can win. Asking them who they think they can be as big as. There isn't one contestant who hasn't seen the show before they enter, so they know what they're getting themselves into, yet most of them stand there as if they'd been asked to multiply 347 by 93. Eventually out they trot with the same old names: Mariah Carey, The Spice Girls, Westlife. Any mention of Westlife or Boyzone is an attempt to get Louis on their side. Equally, any mention of Ozzy is invented (and guaranteed) to get my vote. Usually it's nothing so subtle. Rather than talent, they seem to think all they need is a good sob story to push them through: their grandmother's got a hip operation coming up. They've got one kidney and are on dialysis. Their cat's just died and they're here for Puss. In that first week in London we had one whose horse had just died. Puh-lease.

Then there are the time-wasters who are doing it just for a bet. The producers try to weed those out before we get to see them. But some of them get through. Just a piss-take. They can't use the footage, no matter how bad they are. (And they always are.) Viewers only see perhaps 50 per cent of what we sit through. They see the best and the worst. The other 50 per cent are just plain mediocre and, believe me, that's more exhausting. You try to say something that won't cripple these people for life, yet at the same time you can't afford to give them hope.

What is it with kids? They think all they have to do is turn up and open their mouth and they're entitled to instant fame. And they come out with classic lines like, 'I've worked all my life for this moment', and the majority of them are under twenty! Give me an eighty-year-old woman singing Edith Piaf out of her nose any day.

It's a miracle. Only seven o'clock and we've wrapped. And we're in need of fun. Trish tells us that Harvey Nichols is having its sale and its preview. It's just around the corner from the hotel and it's open until ten.

Word quickly gets around. Silvana, Dannii, Claire – one of the producers – Louis, Simon, me and Patricia, of course, all eager for a bargain. And off we go. All of us ladies end up in the VIP shopping area drinking pink champagne and eating canapés, with assistants running around for us. Luxury! I think we arrived back at the hotel at five to ten. End of a perfect day.

201

# Hollywood

The Belmont aren't sure if they can give Don the care he needs any more. We may have to move him. Another decision I have to make. Sometimes it feels as if I get a call every day – what treatment should we give him; we might need to change his medication, what do you think; should we do this, should we do that? Every day a new question. Sometimes it can feel very lonely, with all this responsibility. And in the middle of it all I'm working on two TV shows and trying to run one of the biggest rock festivals. Crazy. There's never enough time.

I learned so much from my father. And he could be so tough. He had to be. He was only fourteen when he first took to the stage. When he started out there was so much prejudice. A stage manager once called him a 'fucking Jew boy'. My dad punched him. Then proceeded to get banned for two years from a whole bunch of theatres.

Later the violence was more about power. It was absolutely normal to behave that way. If someone looks at you the wrong way, grab them by the neck and choke them – it's fine. That's what people do. Take them to a forest and put a shotgun to their kneecaps if they don't do what you want.

He learned early on how to use violence. He liked the fact that people were afraid of him. But it was the anti-Semitism he was fighting in those early days. It made him tough.

And he was such a pioneer in his heyday. When he was touring he would put on his own shows: summer seasons in Blackpool and Margate. He knew the importance of getting the right balance of acts – something I still do when I put Ozzfest together. Different kind of show, but it's the same principle. He taught me that in order to stay alive in this business you have to keep moving. You have to be creative – come up with fresh ideas.

I rejected the violence, but I'll never forget what I learned from him. There's always competition so you have to keep raising your game. And now Ozzy and I are shaking things up ourselves with Ozzfest.

# 9

## From Russia With Love

Like practically every other musician I have ever known, Ozzy used to believe that inspiration lay in the bottom of a bottle or a Ziploc bag full of coke, and that without being drunk or stoned he couldn't write. That kind of thinking so easily becomes a self-fulfilling prophecy. Since *Down To Earth* was released in 2002 there had been no new album (apart from the covers album, *Under Cover*, in 2005) and Ozzy's confidence was on the floor. He was scared. Scared that he had lost it. Scared that only with some kind of stimulant could he get his creative juices flowing again. Scared to go forward. Scared to go back. He was totally stuck.

You need a certain kind of security to write, and it hadn't helped that in 2002 I got sick with colon cancer and it was no secret that my chances of pulling through were less than 50 per cent. At that point in his life Ozzy was swallowing pills every day, and would get the staff to bring him in beer to help swig them down. Then we had Jack to worry about: not only did we discover that our seventeen-year-old son was an addict, but both we and he had to deal with it in public. (In the end it was Jack and his extraordinary will power in coping with his addiction that gave Ozzy the courage and strength to give sobriety another try.)

Finally, around the beginning of 2006, my husband began to write again. His guitar player Zakk Wylde laid down some riffs and Ozzy would pick them up and build a song round them. Zakk happened to be on tour with his own band, B.L.S., at the time and there was no pressure from the record company to deliver by a certain date, no one calling up and saying, 'Well, how's it going, Oz?' Ozzy had the space to be creative in his own way, and it worked.

In the past, it was always hideous for me when album time came round. It had to be done – albums and the tours that go with them are what make the money in the music business, and in any case it's what Ozzy does, he is a truly creative person and he has to write and make music. He couldn't be any other way. But even so I would dread it: the mind games and the arguments that were a traditional part of the process. But this time it was different. Ozzy had been clean and sober for almost two years at this point, and this time around my role was a kind of nurturing one, and as soon as Ozzy started to write, my job was to encourage. 'That's fantastic,' I would tell him as he would try something out on me. 'That's amazing.' To be frank, it was amazing that he was writing at all and I wanted him to feel that he was producing stuff that was great, spurring him on until gradually – as he began to feel good about himself – it became true, and then I knew there'd be no stopping him. In fact, it's what always happens. The first few tryouts go on the back burner and the newer songs get better and better.

*Black Rain* was released in May and was soon being hailed, by both the fans and the music press, as the best Ozzy had done in years, and within hours we knew he had a hit. A month later, for the first time in his forty-year career, 'I Don't Wanna Stop' became the No. 1 rock single in America.

But even before that monumental achievement, we had already got the industry and music press buzzing. The sixth of February 2007 was a big day for Ozzy, for me and for the history of rock and roll in America. At a press conference in Los Angeles, Ozzy got up from his seat and with a spray gun of black paint, the kind usually used by graffiti artists, wrote the word 'FREE' across the Ozzfest logo at the back of the stage. It was greeted with a mass gasp, then – after a moment's stunned silence – cheers and applause. Nothing like this was expected. Nothing like this had ever happened before.

Planning for the next year's Ozzfest starts in the autumn.

Just enough time, after the final venue, for everyone to take a break and generally calm down. The line-up of any show depends on a combination of budget and who is available. The only given for Ozzfest is Ozzy – after that it's like a menu. He's the main course, then you start thinking about the side dishes, the starters and the rest of it.

Over the last couple of years Ozzy has been taking it easy. At the end of Ozzfest 2005 he announced he wouldn't be appearing the next year at all. In the end he changed his mind, but at the 2006 Ozzfest he performed only on the second stage. He loved it. It was great for the audience to see Ozzy up close, and great for him to have that intimate contact with his fans. He said it took him back to the early days of his career. He was performing at four-thirty in the afternoon, something he had never done on a tour. But in 2007, with *Black Rain* coming out, he would be headlining the main stage again.

Putting together the programme in autumn 2006, we decided Marilyn Manson would be great to have on the tour. We have known him right from the beginning of his career. We had had him on Ozzfest twice before and he is a great showman, one of the music industry's true originals. Whether you like his music or not, he is always intriguing.

Now Marilyn's agent is CAA, the same CAA we left after the Iron Maiden incident. So I'm not at the top of their list. But business is business, and I call them up and tell them we're interested in Marilyn for Ozzfest 2007.

'Well,' the agent goes, 'he's been offered Family Values.'

Another tour. 'And he's also planning on doing his own tour, with a band called Evanescence.' But that wasn't to say he couldn't do Ozzfest, he added. Nothing was settled. 'It all depends who comes in with the highest offer.'

And suddenly the red light goes on and I'm like, I'm not going there, I refuse to go there, I will not get into a bidding war over an artist again. Bollocks. I am not playing this game any more.

The world of music promotion is like any other product or service. Pricing is everything. If your product is too expensive for its potential customers, they won't buy. Ozzfest's audience are kids, they are not media moguls or captains of industry, and you can't charge them the same kind of prices that you would for a Pink Floyd concert. They simply couldn't afford to come. You'd be left with empty arenas and bills that would bankrupt you.

For years now the Ozzfest line-up has totalled in the region of twenty-one bands. Some of these are unsigned bands that don't demand a fortune, but it all adds up, and if you start paying ridiculous money at the top, then the ticket price has to cover this, otherwise we would not be in business.

When Ozzfest started, in 1995, we were the only game in town. There was nowhere else you could go to hear hard-edge music, and nowhere else the bands could play. That's why I started the festival in the first place, because there was no other tour for Ozzy to join. But it hasn't stayed that way. Like any other business, you find a niche, you make it successful, and some other motherfucker comes in and copies you. So it has proved with Ozzfest. From zero hard-edged festivals in the mid-nineties, to now, thirteen years on, there are three or four out there – not as big as Ozzfest, but a mosquito can cause more trouble than an elephant – and there aren't enough bands to go round. Competition is a fact of commercial life and I accept that. But I am a businesswoman and experience has taught me that if something isn't working, it has to change.

Put simply, the cake is getting smaller, and the way this is being played out is that agents are demanding more and more for their clients, which is part of their jobs of course, but I'm wearing my producer's hat, so it's not good for me. It reaches a point where you can't feed the machine you've created. As for the economics of our tour: we are not a small-scale operation. We employ twenty-one bands, and play twenty-six venues across America over an eight-week period. Meanwhile the cost of everything is going up: the cost of trucking, the cost of fuel, the cost of renting the venues. Everybody has to be fed: four hundred meals a day. Then there are the riders. Riders are what bands expect in addition to their fee; it's like a wish list that the promoter has to fulfil. Some of these are basic to everybody: clean towels, water, basic food. Some, coming from the top bands, are totally ridiculous, from fine wines to sushi.

As expenses go up, so do ticket prices – it's a vicious circle – and our audience don't have the money. You reach the point where you price yourself out of the market.

And that's exactly what's been happening. Year on year, the take has been diminishing. Ticket sales are 25 per cent down on where we were five years ago. Ozzfest had become like a two-headed monster and we couldn't earn enough to feed it. With the catering, with the crew, with the union crew, there was no profit. In 2005 Iron Maiden were taking home a profit of $185,000 a show. In 2006 System of a Down took home $325,00 a show. We were taking home no profit.

We just got tired of it, tired of going home every year with no profit, and you think: people are taking the piss. The band managements are taking the piss. The agents are taking the piss. They know there are only so many acts on these summer tours, and they're ratcheting it up. Now they've gone to bidding wars. Well, I'm not. I'm bailing. I'm not bidding on any motherfucker. Not even for Marilyn Manson.

I could have got out. I could have held up my hands, waved the white flag and said: That's it. I give up. Give myself a break from this head-banging, get a life, and go to the beach for the summer. But that's not me. Plus I have to look at it as a business venture. We have created a brand and I don't want to lose that brand. I have to keep the brand going because it's sound business sense. Ozzy's got a new record coming out, the first in six years. And, more importantly, we don't want to let the fans down. They still want to go to Ozzfest, so I'll just have to do it a different way.

I can't remember exactly when we made the decision: that's it, we're not going to pay and we're not going to charge a penny, and any band that wants to come, can come. But we did. And that, basically, was the deal, the formula we came up with. My bottom line was: I don't care if you sell a hundred records or a hundred thousand or a million records. You come, you play. I'll give you a stage, I'll give you a place to sell your merchandise, I'll give you an audience. You come if you want, and that's the way we left it.

So how does it work? How can we afford to pay for the infrastructure, the rent, the security, the first-aid workers, the crew, the union crews, the food?

Sponsorship. You get sponsors to come in and they under-write the tour. Exactly like big sporting events, they get access to a core market. Energy drinks, beer, sportswear, condoms, computer games. You name it. They want all the information they can get about our audience, from their age to what colour socks they're wearing, to how often they buy a new truck or send their mother flowers – and that is worth a for-tune in today's world.

Meanwhile, the bands get to sell their T-shirts and their CDs – all their merchandise – to huge numbers of people. Plus they can earn money on their days off, individual gigs here and there along the route, that's fine. They can charge for those, take 100 per cent of the turnstile. But what they want above all is to play and to sell their merchandise to full houses, and that we can give them.

And, best of all, the fans still get to see a wide number of hard-edge, fantastic bands – and all for free.

It wasn't that radical an idea. Free concerts have been around for a long time. Bob Dylan, the Rolling Stones – there have been plenty of examples over the years. Central Park, New York, is always having them. Every single one is funded by sponsorship. I already understood about sponsorship and how it worked. We'd had sponsors right from the beginning of Ozzfest, but never to such a degree.

Over the autumn of 2006 we did the sums and, when I could see that the business model was viable, I spoke to Marsha, who is far more than just our agent. Marsha is one of my oldest friends, I've known her since before Ozzy and I were married when we were both that unusual thing, young women working in the male-only world of the music industry. She's a true New Yorker. Skeleton-thin and sharp as they come, peroxided hair and big black glasses. The Marsha Vlasic Organisation is a small boutique agency and has people like Neil Young and Elvis Costello, Morrissey and The Strokes.

I could hear the huge intake of breath on the other end of the phone when I explained what I wanted to do.

'You're crazy,' she said in that great New Yorker accent. 'You're crazy. You're out of your fucking mind.' After she'd calmed down, I talked her through it, and finally into it. 'But I warn you,' she said. 'You're going to have a lot of shtick.'

She was right. The Queens of the Stone Age weren't the only people who used it as an opportunity to stick the knife in. Nor was it easy for her. The first people she would need to convince that a Free Ozzfest made business sense were Live Nation, who own all the venues. Live Nation is such a huge presence in the touring market and come what may, she has to work with them with all her other clients. But here we were lucky.

Mike Rapino, a young Canadian who's president of the company, was 100 per cent behind us. As he sees it, if his facilities are full then he's making money on the parking and the beer. They don't make their money because Ozzy is going in and selling out, or Aerosmith, or Fred Bloggs. They make money on concessions and that's all they care about. The original guy that owned the company was Bob Sillerman. When we signed with him twelve years ago, I said, 'Have you ever been to an Ozzy concert?' He goes, 'Fuck no. I don't give a fuck what your husband sounds like, what he sings, all I know is that his audience drink my beer and that's all I give a fuck about.' I said, 'I love you too, give me the cheque and I'm out of here.' There was no bullshit, no wining and dining. It was: how much do you want for Ozzfest? I told him. Done. That's what it's all about. Our audience drink their beer.

Although Live Nation stood by us, a lot of powerful people turned against us and wanted us to fail. Top of the list were the agents. If a free Ozzfest works, then the whole house of cards could come crashing down around their Prada suits. So these agents put pressure on their big clients – huge pressure – not to do the tour, and right from when the penny first dropped about what it was going to mean, people have been stabbing us in the back. It was the same with the press. We can't fight the major agencies, we're not big enough. We can't compete.

The reality is that most of the people we deal with wouldn't lose out. Like Bob Sillerman saw only too clearly, the promoters would still be getting the things that count for them: the car parking, a huge percentage of the alcohol, their food and their T-shirts, which is where all the money is made. But people in the recording industry don't like change, which is why it is in the toilet. That's what I mean about my father being a pioneer. In the sixties and seventies he shook things up in this industry and people didn't like it. Now the same thing was happening again. Everyone was burying their heads in the sand. They didn't see that the world was changing with the internet and downloading. The people that run the recording industry were blind, deaf and dumb. A whole generation grew up on the computer while they were looking the other way.

So the industry threw shit at us and some of it stuck. 'You'll get the bottom of the barrel . . . you'll get the dregs . . . no one who could afford to buy a ticket will come if it's free. It'll be mayhem . . . there'll be riots.'

One early casualty among potential sponsors was PlayStation. They have been sponsoring us for years but this year they backed out. I understand. If you are an advertising agency and you are investing other people's money, you have to play safe, especially with huge clients like PlayStation. Who knew what would happen? They weren't prepared to put their million dollars with us.

Then there was Camel. Mike Rapino was keen for this to work. So he calls me up and says that Camel cigarettes want to be a sponsor, to come and put up a tent and give out free cigarettes. Now on a personal level I wasn't overjoyed about that, but there was huge pressure from Live Nation and they've been good to us, so I agreed to a conference call to discuss it with the advertising company, Camel themselves and the sponsorship department from Live Nation. Straight off the advertising company start firing questions at me. 'What calibre of bands are you going to get if you're not paying them? What calibre of people are you going to get if they don't have to pay? Don't you think it's demeaning giving music away free?'

This was the first time I had heard this particular line and I was bemused.

'Why would it be demeaning? Music has always been free. You turn on the radio, you don't pay. You can listen to music twenty-four hours a day. You can download music. You can go into an elevator, or a restaurant or a shop, and hear music for free. Some of the great music events of all time have been free: Bob Dylan in the park, Simon and Garfunkel. The Rolling Stones have given free concerts.'

'So you don't think you're going to get young children going to the concert because it's free?'

'No,' I said, and then I blew. 'Look, Ozzy has been an innovator for forty years. He changed the face of music, he changed the face of television, he is a proven entity, he has a fan base other people would kill for. People have been coming to see him for forty years, why should they stop now? They will still keep coming. We're not saying: the gate's open, come in. You will have a ticket, the only difference is you will be providing information rather than cash. We will know exactly how many people are coming. It will not be a scrum at the door.'

The reason we have always done Ozzfest in a venue is that I have never wanted to go into a field. I have always taken these shows into a structured facility so you can have security. Security for the artists as well as for the audience. And then I lost it.

'You know what? You're all wankers. You know nothing about this fucking industry, so don't fucking question me about how to handle an audience. I don't fucking question you about what the fuck you put in your cigarettes. Don't question me about what artist I'm having on my stage. You're talking to me because I'm an expert in what I do. I'm talking to you because you're experts in fucking killing kids. Don't try and fucking belittle me or put me in a corner. You're a fucking cigarette company. I have no respect for you. I don't even know who you are, you're faceless, nameless people. So go fuck yourselves.'

That was the end of the conversation. They all hung up. I was still in mid-rant.

When he heard what had happened, Mike Rapino was livid. He couldn't believe what I had said to these people.

'Sharon, you are insane. You are in business. What are you doing treating people like this?'

'I don't have to prove what I do to some prick that puts a product on the market that kills people. Am I meant to be bowing and scraping for this twat just so he can give cigarettes away at my gig for a million dollars? You should be fucking convincing me that what I'm doing is not a fucking sin.

I felt utterly exhilarated: it was like high fives all the way. Did they honestly think I was prepared to kow-tow to cigarette manufacturers and say, 'You know what? Yes, Ozzy will go into your tent, smoking your cigarettes. I'll have him go on stage with a cigarette hanging out of his mouth like Keith Richards'?

Because if I had gone down that route, that's what they would have wanted me to do.

'Would Ozzy come into our tent?'

'No, Ozzy doesn't smoke. Are you mad?'

People like the Rolling Stones can do that, because they truly do smoke. We don't. And these guys, they honestly thought that I was going to be licking dick. Saying, 'Oh, I'll get Ozzy in the tent, and maybe I could make him wear a Camel T-shirt on stage. Or perhaps you'd like him to stick a cigarette up his arse.'

There are problems with sponsorship, and it's by no means the licence to print money it might seem. In the past we've been lucky, we've had sponsors who reflect the core audience demographic. We've had high-energy drinks, we've had Jack Daniel's, we've had Jägermeister.

I'm not apologetic about having alcohol sponsors. People drink, I drink. Ozzy doesn't drink. Ozzy has never had a photo taken with a Jägermeister. It would never happen in a million years. But Ozzy's fans do like to drink, and God bless them. It just so happens that Ozzy is an alcoholic, he can't drink it. But you know what? Most people can.

We lost so many sponsors. I'd get them on the phone:

'Oh, we hear it's going to be a nightmare.'

'Why?'

'Because it's free.'

'But you give your drinks away free at the shows, is that a nightmare?'

'No . . .'

We even lost Trojan, a fucking condom company.

So this was what we announced on 6 February. Ozzfest 2007 would be free. The fans were delighted. The industry less so, partly because they were jealous they hadn't got in there first, and partly because the agents are an important lobby and they would be the losers. In 2006 CAA had four or five bands on Ozzfest, and 10 per cent of the fees went to them. They were earning a fortune, so of course they were pissed off. If it worked, then the writing was on the wall. However, in my view agents should see it as a challenge rather than a threat. It's about being creative. It's no longer enough to say: You want my artist, then you have to pay obscene amounts of money. It's no longer good enough just booking a band into this venue and that venue. If they had any sense agents would be identifying appropriate sponsors for their artists. American Express, Red Bull, PlayStation, Visa – these people want tours to underwrite. In the past it was just a handful of superstar artists who could get sponsors to underwrite their tours. No longer. Information is a valuable commodity today. *The* valuable commodity. If I was Ford and in the business of selling trucks, then I'd want access to a heavy metal audience. If I was MAC make-up, then I'd be thinking of a Fergie tour. Names and numbers and email addresses are worth a fortune and that's what the future is all about.

A new album always means a tour: first Europe till the end of June, then back to America for Ozzfest, starting in Seattle on 12 July and then a switchback across the country from coast to coast, north to south. A month off in September, then Europe again, moving onto Australia and finally Japan and the Far East. Ending not far short of my husband's sixtieth birthday in December 2008.

Whenever possible, I try to be there to see Ozzy perform, as I have always done, wherever he is. If I can't physically be there, we always speak before he goes on stage and when he comes off. It doesn't matter where he is in the world, or where I am, or what the time difference. We speak.

And it was exciting, especially as the European tour started in Russia. Ozzy had played there eighteen years before, at the Moscow Peace Festival in 1989. Two years later the Soviet Union was no more, but when we were there it was still heavy-duty communist. In fact, some people have said that this festival played a part in the ending of the Cold War. (That being said, David Hasselhoff once famously claimed that one of his songs helped bring down the Berlin wall so . . . you know.) Moscow was the first time Ozzy performed the new album live. What a great place to start his world tour.

It had certainly been a different world back in 1989. Ozzy hadn't really wanted to go. Modern history – particularly Russia and the Revolution leading up to the Second World War – is his passion, and, knowing so much about it, communism had always frightened him. The festival was being run by Doc McGhee, the manager of Bon Jovi and Mötley Crüe. I had known him for many years – he's charming and persuasive, and he needed all of that to get Ozzy to agree.

Even though our babies were still quite small, I was determined not to miss out. Ten days was a long time, however. I had a nanny, but I made it a rule never to leave them alone with her for more than a couple of days. So I flew my niece Gina and her then husband to Los Angeles and installed them at Malibu, where we were living in a little rented house on the beach, to keep an eye on my precious ones.

The festival was in aid of international cooperation to fight drug addiction – the height of irony considering the majority of those involved were on just about everything. Nevertheless, the money raised was going towards building rehabilitation centres in the Soviet Union, as it then was. What a load of old bollocks.

It was a big deal. MTV, then a brand new set-up, were covering it pay-per-view. It was the first time anything like this had been done behind the Iron Curtain. Yes, other musicians had played there before, but not heavy metal and never on this scale. By any standards, the line-up was impressive: Ozzy, Mötley Crüe, Skid Row, Cinderella, The Scorpions and Bon Jovi. There was also a Russian band called Gorky Park. Bon Jovi were headlining. At that time they were very big in America and that's where MTV's audience was, so fair enough.

We flew from Newark, New Jersey, on a jet chartered by the Make A Difference Foundation. All the artists were on it – about two hundred and fifty people, including press, wives and girlfriends. We landed at Stansted to pick up The Scorpions, a German band, then it was non-stop to Moscow.

There was a real buzz on the plane, mostly the excitement of going somewhere so different. But the organisers would have been horrified at the amount of drink and drugs being consumed. It should have been called Hypocrites Anonymous. The bottom line was pretty much nobody gave a fuck about why we were going. Most people just wanted to go to Russia and be on MTV. Including us.

We landed at the main Moscow airport and because they were so unused to foreign visitors, from then on we were treated like diplomats. They took our passports. (We saw them once more at the hotel when we were given ID cards, then that was the last we saw of them until we left.) Airports are much the same wherever you are in the world, but Moscow Airport was a shock. Along the tarmac we could see carcasses of old planes, left by the side of the runway to rot.

On the drive into the centre of Moscow you immediately saw how run-down everything was, from the state of the road itself to the houses alongside, which were more like wooden shacks. Although they looked like farm outbuildings, the interpreter said it was where the workers lived. Once in the city itself, there was nothing but grey tower blocks, all with tiny windows, all of them about eight storeys high, all exactly the same. They were the ugliest-looking buildings I had ever seen. Everything in Moscow was grey, a grey concrete jungle with no trees, no green at all. Even the sky was grey. Ozzy and I stopped talking we were so shocked. Although we had always known it would be different, it was worse than anything you could ever see in Britain, even in the worst bits of London or Glasgow. Utterly colourless and no sign of life anywhere.

We heard later that there were very few hotels that foreigners could stay at in the whole of Russia. The main Moscow one was called the Ukraine. It was huge. Each floor had well over a hundred rooms. In the plane Doc warned us to watch what we said. 'The rooms,' he told us, 'will probably be bugged.' We thought he was joking. I mean, what kind of information would a bunch of crazy musicians have to offer? Most of them were so out of their skulls that whatever they said would be unintelligible anyway, not least to a Russian. Once we'd been there a few days, however, we realised it was true. Even the interpreters had recorders, and everything we said to them was taped.

The hotel was horrendous, like the worst government building you could imagine, everything dark and dingy and depressing, and the lobby stank of urine. Smell was obviously a big thing: everywhere we went, people would come up and sniff Ozzy and me. They didn't have soap or perfume, and Ozzy and I are always drenched in it.. The ID cards we were issued with had your name in English and Russian, passport number and room number. There were about twenty floors in this hotel and each floor had its own guard. You'd come out of the lift and there in front of you was a desk with a woman who kept the keys. Before handing them over, she'd check your ID card, and mark down anybody who was with you. She would also give out sheets of toilet paper to those poor sods who hadn't had the wit to bring their own. Ours looked like Rosa Klebb in *From Russia With Love*. Her English was non-existent. Everything was *da* and *niet*. Mostly *niet*. She was quite obviously a member of the KGB.

The other permanent inhabitant on our floor was the cleaner. She had a little room off the corridor and was dressed just like you would think a Russian peasant would dress: the shapeless skirt and top, apron and headscarf, flat black shoes and thick wool stockings, even though it was midsummer.

Our bedroom was like I imagine a fifties youth hostel might have been: bleak and minimal. By this point Ozzy had completely lost the power of speech – he pointed at the bed, which I then realised was two singles pushed together. As for the bathroom, it was perfectly clean, though our towels were the size of drying-up cloths. No soap, naturally. Luckily we'd been warned and brought our own, ditto toilet paper. One suitcase was completely filled with the stuff we'd been advised to bring. As well as soap and loo roll there were cigarettes, jeans, cassettes, T-shirts and toothpaste. Ozzy's current tour was *No Rest For The Wicked* and we must have brought a thousand cassettes of that and his first two albums. The T-shirts were left over from the American tour so they had American dates on them.

We barely had time to dump our bags before we were hustled off to the press conference, which was held in the Ministry of Foreign Affairs, one of those massive buildings that you see on TV with soldiers standing outside and politicians in fur hats and suits going in and out. Not that there were any fur hats around when we were there. It was August, grey but hot. The room itself looked like the chamber of the UN, with tiers of desks rising up like an amphitheatre. It was huge, with enough space for about five hundred journalists. On the stage you got the singer from each band plus somebody from the management. Ozzy went up and I went with him.

The majority of the press were Russian, but a few American journalists were there who had been with us on the plane, plus some based in Europe who had come in on commercial flights.

The way it all happened took everyone by surprise. I don't think anybody but me and Doc McGhee had done any kind of press conference in their lives, let along something this bizarre. As for the questions themselves from the local Russian press, they were what you would expect: how pleased are you to be in the Soviet Union; what songs are you going to play? What no one expected was that 80 per cent of them would be directed at Ozzy. He was the one they wanted. Bon Jovi – who was headlining – was too new and his work had not yet reached Russia.

It turned out that Black Sabbath was an underground cult. As records from the West were not legally available, there were no sales to provide any kind of clue as to what the fan base might be.

After the press conference there was a general photo session, then it was back to the hotel. For the first time Ozzy and I lay down on the bed. The mattress was about two inches thick and made of horsehair. Each one had a huge dip in the middle where it had been worn away. You felt like you were lying on a packet of crisps.

All the catering was down at the stadium. Doc had said that we should eat nothing at the hotel or anywhere else. Everything had been brought in on huge trucks, from the water to the food to the cleaning materials. So for breakfast, lunch and dinner we had to go down to the stadium. The food was good, done by English caterers called Eat Your Hearts Out. The transport had all been brought in from Germany but it was run by an English team with CB radios, and there were regular shuttles between the hotel and the stadium. If we wanted to go anywhere else, then it had to be with an interpreter, and as for trying to hail a taxi, you held out your hand with a red carton of Marlboro cigarettes and five would stop. If you tipped it had to be with cigarettes. Money meant nothing.

The first morning I woke up with a start to hear Ozzy shouting, 'What the fuck!', and opened my eyes to see an entire TV crew standing at the bottom of the bed. There was a cameraman, a soundman and a lighting man standing with a light bulb held above his head – the kind of thing you take up to the attic. Then a young girl behind the camera began asking questions very politely, starting with, 'So what does it feel like, Mr Osbourne, to be in Russia?'

I put my head under the cover and was absolutely cracking up while Ozzy screamed down the phone to Tony in the next room.

Somehow Tony managed to move them outside, then he found our interpreter. The film crew were from the main Moscow TV company, she explained, and the hotel staff had let them into our room using a pass key.

'But you can't just walk into a bedroom without permission!' he said.

'But permission we have! This for the biggest TV station in Russia! We must do interview!'

He came back to us for instructions. 'Sure we'll do the interview,' we told him. 'Say they can come back later at the time we decide to do it.' They wouldn't leave. They waited outside in the corridor all day.

Eventually we emerged and gave them their interview. In reply to the question, 'So, Mrs Osbourne, how does it feel to be in Russia?' I said, 'Great, except for waking up to find a film crew standing at the bottom of the bed.'

Back then, the Lenin stadium was the biggest in Russia and seated 85,000 – roughly the same size as Wembley. It had never been used for a rock concert before, so nobody knew how many the central area would hold – at least another 15,000, making the capacity a nice round hundred thousand.

We were there in total for ten days and we did two shows. Looking back, Ozzy should have been headlining. He was the one the kids all wanted to see.

Doc McGhee had told me the line-up was going to be Bon Jovi, The Scorpions, Ozzy and then Mötley Crüe. It soon became clear, however, that we had all been given different stories: Mötley Crüe said that Doc McGhee had promised them Ozzy's slot, and it ended up in a huge fight with Tommy Lee punching Doc in the face. For us it was a particularly difficult situation because Tommy and Mötley Crüe were a huge part of our lives.

We first met them in San Bernardino in 1983 when they

opened the US festival there. They hadn't yet had an album released but there was a huge underground vibe about them. They were very young, and I remember that I was pregnant with Aimee. When I saw them I said to Tommy Lee, 'I'm going to take you on tour with Ozzy.' And that's what happened. It was the year after Randy Rhoads died and Ozzy needed to be taken out of himself. Tommy was like his kid brother. They were all of them crazy kids and they encouraged Ozzy to be crazier than he was – if you've got a partner in crime it's worse. It was a difficult time for me. By then Aimee had been born and I was pregnant with Kelly, and they would disappear for days at a time, all of them together. They were like pirates, but nicely so. They weren't mean, they were having the time of their life, young, single, successful. We loved them, they loved us. I was the one telling them off. Like a headmistress. Once they had T-shirts printed with a non-smiley face and the words: The No-Fun Tour. The non-smiley face was me. It was all laughter and tears and craziness. They were like naughty younger brothers.

Although they all came from California, once we were back in LA, Tommy was the one we latched onto. He adored the children, all of them. One of the first pictures of Aimee I ever put up was him and Ozzy holding her in their hands.

He had great likeability. He would come into a room and light it up. He was this great tall lolloping thing, covered with tattoos, and you would instantly be smitten with him. I see him now in his forties but he's still a little boy to me, a naughty, lovable little boy, and through all his ups and downs in his life we would always support Tommy.

The first thing we knew about the trouble in Moscow was when Doc came to find us in the dressing room.

'Ozzy,' he said, 'I've got a favour to ask. Will you switch with Mötley Crüe?'

'Are you crazy?' said Ozzy. 'No.' Friends they might be, but we still thought of them as our support band.

'Look, I'll do anything for you, if only you'll do it,' Doc went on.

'Anything?'

'Anything.'

'Whatever I want?' said Ozzy, increasingly incredulous.

'Whatever you want.'

There were rumours on the tour that the American doctor Doc had brought in was holding the coke.

'What about coke?' Ozzy said.

'You gottit.'

Ozzy laughed out loud. 'You've got to be fucking joking! No fucking way am I doing coke in Russia.' We were just testing him.

Doc left the room and nothing further needed to be said.

Ozzy really wasn't bothered about the line-up because he was so clearly the star of the festival. Everybody in the audience had banners: Ozzy, we love you. Ozzy, thanks for coming. It was an amazing atmosphere, considering the whole place was ringed with soldiers three deep, all of them armed and in full uniform. There must have been several thousand. At the front of the stadium alone there were over two hundred. There were girls in the crowd sitting on boys' shoulders and waving, and one of these girls, who was clearly mad for Ozzy, lifted up her shirt and flashed her tits. Suddenly these soldiers grabbed her, pulled her off the guy's shoulders and dragged her round to the back of the stage and about three of them started to beat her in full view of everyone on stage.

Ozzy saw, we all saw. I was horrified, quickly found the interpreter and said, 'You can't do that!' Then I found Doc. He just put his hands in the air.

'Sorry, Sharon,' he said. 'I can do many things, but I can't tell the Russian army what to do.'

Every day Tony would take down boxes of cassettes and T-shirts to the venue, but giving them away was a dangerous business. He told us how, once they realised what was happening, they would rush at him, the boxes would be ripped open and it would turn into a punch-up.

One day when we couldn't be bothered to go down to the stadium to get food, Ozzy asked Tony to bring him back a sandwich. There was a bar just off the lobby and Ozzy had discovered Russian vodka. So Tony came back with a sandwich, which he'd wrapped in greaseproof paper, and put it on the table where Ozzy's glasses were lined up. A group of us were sitting there chatting while Ozzy was drinking. Eventually he decided he was hungry, picked up the sandwich and was unwrapping the paper when three cockroaches crawled out. Ozzy screamed. The interpreter freaked out. I went as fast as my legs could carry me back to the bedroom. In fact, there were roaches everywhere. We even found some in our luggage when we got home.

By the end of the stay we still had jeans and cigarettes and toothpaste and loo rolls – things we obviously didn't want to take back. The answer was simple. We should give them to the cleaner, the woman who sat in the little room at the end of our corridor where she had her samovar for her tea. She could keep what she wanted and sell the rest.

So the next time she came in our room, Ozzy tried to hand over this stuff, but she kept saying *niet*, *niet*, pointing with one finger at the ceiling, the other finger across her mouth, at the same time jerking her head towards the door. She was panicked, obviously scared that the room was bugged. So I said to Ozzy, 'Leave it half an hour, then go to her room and give it to her there.'

So he packed up a suitcase with this stuff and after twenty minutes or so went out. Next thing I knew he came running back.

'Oh my God,' he shouted, 'that's the last time you get me to do your dirty work!' Unable to see her through the door, he'd gone in, walked round the corner and found her sitting on the toilet with her knickers down, having a crap.

'Come on,' I said. 'We'll both go back and do it.' So this poor woman – who was by now drinking the old tea – couldn't believe it when we handed over the suitcase filled with all this stuff. Her eyes welled up. It was sad to see these people then. They were crying over the food we occasionally managed to give them. We saw no dogs and no cats in Russia. No birds either. Eventually we realised they must kill them to eat.

One night we had just come back from the stadium after the show, when one of the interpreters knocked at our door very out of breath. Ozzy had to come downstairs, she said. Straight away. She couldn't really explain any more. As soon as we entered the lobby I could hear this loud hum, like bees swarming. The entrance to the hotel was crowded with people, not moving, just staring out into the night, which seemed unusually bright.

Then we heard the noise of chanting: Ozzy, Ozzy, Ozzy. We pushed our way through the crowd and onto the steps leading up to the hotel. There, in the street, were about two hundred motorcyclists dressed in black. They were Russia's equivalent of Hell's Angels, who had come to the hotel to pay tribute to Ozzy. They looked nothing like the American or even English Hell's Angels because the motorbikes were so old, like things you'd have got in the Second World War. Of course he went out and signed autographs and did pictures with them, and Tony went back to the room to get T-shirts and cassettes. For me, seeing Ozzy standing there among these guys, the engines humming, the lights shining through the dark Moscow street, was one of the most moving things of the whole extraordinary experience.

At the end of the ten days, everybody was ready to go, and

when the plane took off we all applauded. It had been fantastic but it was a great relief to be going home.


Eighteen years on and Russia was a whole other place. Only Tony and Zakk Wylde had been with us that first time, and we felt quite differently from the others, excited in a way they couldn't begin to understand.

We arrived on 27 May, and from the moment we landed it was incredible. I have no idea what kind of cars they put us in before, but they were definitely not Mercedes. Camera crews were waiting at the airport and there were even paparazzi outside the hotel. Not, thank God, the Ukraine, but the Hotel Intercontinental, which has to be one of the best hotels I have ever stayed in. Beautiful from the lobby upwards. Fantastic service, a twenty-four-hour bar – you don't even get that in London. The first person I recognised walking across the lobby was Yoko Ono. It felt utterly surreal.

Our suite was enormous – about four times the size of the room we'd had before, beautifully done out: B & O stereo system, flat screen, DVD, all of that, the bathroom all marble and chrome, and our balcony looked right across the rooftops to Red Square, where you could just see the cross at the top of St Basil's Cathedral.

Everyone else on the tour took it for granted. For them it was just another city, just another gig. But for Ozzy and me – and probably for Tony and Zakk too – it was incredible. The thing that surprised us most was that we could walk wherever we wanted! From our balcony we could see this rainbow collection of flags in Red Square, so we thought we'd just go over and take a look, perhaps have a cup of coffee in one of the cafés we'd heard about. When we got there we discovered to our astonishment that there was a demonstration going on – hundreds of people – and what's more, they were all shouting in English.

Then I saw Richard Fairbrass – one of the guys from Right Said Fred – talking to a crowd of what were clearly gay activists. So instead of Ozzy and me sitting quietly in a café playing at being tourists, we found ourselves in the middle of a bloody riot, because just as we arrived the police moved in and started baton-charging and bashing people about. It was horrible. Nobody intervened to help. They just let it happen. We got out of there sooner than you can say 'I'm too sexy'.

We found out later that it was a Gay Pride march that the mayor of Moscow had banned, and that a thousand police had been drafted in to deal with it. Although the law to decriminalise homosexuality was passed at the same time as the Iron Curtain came down, gay people are still not accepted. And there were we, thinking we would have a coffee and a little *croque-monsieur* and watch the soldiers marching up and down Red Square, and what we got was Right Said Fred getting beaten up.

The local promoter was a woman called Natalya who said we should call her Natalie. She spoke very good English and had worked all her life in the arts. In the days when it was still the Soviet Union, she would take circuses on tour all over the world. Then, when the political climate began to change, she started bringing in Western artists. She has worked with everyone, from Elton downwards.

Although it was only the end of May, Moscow was in the middle of a heat wave. You couldn't believe where that weather was coming from. Shortly after Ozzy and I had retired to the hotel after the gay parade, Natalie phoned up and said, 'It's OK, you can come out now, it's quite safe!' So Silvana and I went back to Red Square, then we got an iced tea before we hit the shopping quarter. Yet again I was amazed. Less than twenty years before, the shops in Moscow were empty. Now the windows were groaning and Muscovites were strolling along, taking as little notice as they would do anywhere else in the world. When it came to shopping, I soon discovered that Natalie was a woman after my own heart.

Although the food in the hotel was wonderful – blinis and caviar every time you ordered a drink – we didn't want to eat in some version of a supper club after the show, we wanted traditional Russian food in a traditional Russian restaurant. So that's what we did, and even in local neighbourhood places the food was fabulous.

As Moscow was the first date on Ozzy's *Black Rain* tour, everyone was a little tense – it was still a work-in-progress at this stage – but the show went really well. The arena was sold out, and Ozzy had the most fantastic reception.

What I found particularly touching was how everyone was so proud of their country and never said anything bad about it, though things are obviously very tough financially for ordinary people.

In 1989 we never went out of Moscow, but this time we flew north to the city that used to be called Leningrad – and that was a very different vibe. Perhaps because of the gay rights business Moscow had felt intense, with police and security everywhere. St Petersburg was much more laid back. The city – the buildings, the way it's all laid out with canals – is breathtakingly gorgeous. We stayed in the Astoria Hotel, a beautifully refurbished old building within walking distance of the Hermitage, though the sightseeing on our day off began in the war museum, which was what Ozzy really wanted to see, and even I had to admit it was fascinating.

In the afternoon we had a private tour of the Hermitage with our interpreter Tasia, short for Anastasia. To be honest, I found it overwhelming. Every single inch of the walls was covered with masterpieces by the greatest artists the world has ever known. Even down to the chandeliers and the china pieces – everything was too much to take in. Although we were there for several hours, really you would need three or four days at least to see it properly. We had the whirlwind tour. Nonetheless it was mind-blowing. You can understand why the Russian peasantry got pissed off because there's so much unimaginable wealth there. It made bloody Buckingham Palace look like something from *Coronation Street*.

St Petersburg is so far north that at that time of the year it hardly gets dark at all – maybe two hours around midnight – and from our window we could see tourists walking around all night.

What a privilege that trip was. So moving. For anyone who never visited Russia when the Iron Curtain was still up, it's hard to explain. It was particularly strange for me, as Don's family are from Georgia, which was part of the Soviet Union until 1991. In any case, for both Ozzy and me, going back was an amazing experience, and one we'll never forget.

In a couple of weeks, Ozzy is set to play Wembley arena. He has just two dates in England this summer, Wembley and Birmingham. Both are really important and we would never do one without the other. Birmingham is Ozzy's home town, and he's always more nervous there than anywhere else, knowing that so many friends and family will be watching him. On 7 July, he's being honoured in Birmingham's brand new Walk of Fame – their very first invitee and I know it's going to be emotional for him. I can't be there as I'll be in Belfast doing more *X-Factor* auditions, but Jackie Boy will be there and Jessica, Ozzy's eldest daughter, and her two little ones, Isabel and Harry. Then there'll be his three sisters and his brother Paul, and any of his nieces and nephews who're around, including, of course, Cousin Terry.

Although he's played it loads of times, Wembley is always a

big deal for Ozzy. London is where we lived for so many years. It's where our children were born. It's where most of our friends still live.

During the whole of last year he did fourteen shows. It's still only June and yet he's done over fourteen already in the last four weeks and we've got eighteen months' solid touring ahead.

You have to have a plan or else you'll drift. My plan is that he'll work until he's sixty and then stop. At least we will be in a position to do what we want to do. We have worked for the right to do so. Ozzy's so lucky, at his age, still to have the following and the reputation and the audiences. It's just incredible. Of the older guys, there are only a handful of performers who have that luxury.

Every night I worry, but every night he's fine. As soon as he's in front of the audience, it's the ultimate high.

# Hollywood

The CD ends and the room is quiet again. I should leave. There's so much to do.

The doctors say they don't think he has long to go. But he's been fighting this illness for ten years and if there's one thing my father and I both share, it's a stubborn streak. How many times have they said, 'We don't think he's going to last more than a few days', and he's pulled through. Over and over.

That's Don. He's always been a fighter. Even now, when he has so little strength left. He'll go out on his own terms.

Sitting here with him, thinking about my life, it's made me realise. I've learned so much from him. The good and the bad. Everything has been a lesson learned.

I have had an unbelievable life. Unbelievable experiences.

I've seen and done things and I look back now . . . incredible. To be a young girl living in LA in the Howard Hughes house, and then the next thing you know the FBI are at the door. I didn't call my first book *Extreme* for nothing.

But I don't want that kind of life any more. All that craziness, the fighting, the betrayal. That was my father's life. The world according to Don. 'You're either with me or you're against me.' He could never let things go. All those feuds – they consumed him. He'll take it all to his grave, that bitterness. And I don't want that.

At least there's one feud he did resolve. It was hard, so hard, but in the end I'm glad he came back into my life six years ago. I'm glad my children got the chance to decide for themselves whether they wanted to meet their grandfather. And I'm glad I can be here for him now, at the end of his life.

I pick up my bag and walk to the door. I turn to look at him one last time, sitting in his wheelchair. He hasn't moved. His expression is still empty. He hasn't changed.

'Bye Dad. I love you.'

I leave the room and head back towards the street. Towards the sunshine.

# 10

---

# Saying Goodbye

For so many years I believed in this whole fictional character my father had created for himself. I guess from the moment he changed his name from Harry Levy to Don Arden, that character was born. He was a performer after all – an actor. And 'Don Arden' was the greatest role he ever played.

When I finally realised he was not the man I thought he was, that's when the split came. It was life-changing for me. I had dared to challenge him, and that was something Don couldn't tolerate. I was no longer his daughter. When we parted, he said I was dead. Dead to him and the whole family. Dead, gone, buried.

I lost my father nearly twenty-six years ago. He was alive,

but he wasn't in my life. I grieved for him then. I can remember going to bed with a pain in the pit of my stomach and waking up with the same pain and thinking, I've lost my father. It was the pain of loss. When you see women wailing on the TV, when they've lost someone – that's how it was for me. I would sit in my bed, rocking and crying. I'd wake up every morning and it would hit me again. I cried for him for years.

There wasn't a day went by when I didn't think about him. I'd see somebody driving a car and they'd have the same hairline and I'd think, God, is it him? I'd see somebody at an airport or walking across the road, and they'd have a similar build to the way I remembered him. Every single day he was on my mind. But I'd never dream of him. None of that slow-motion running-in-a-field-of-daisies chasing-a-puppy thing. He was just in my life.

But then the space closed over. I had Ozzy, I had the kids, I had my friends. My life was full without him. When the kids were growing up I had no one to rely on but myself. Ozzy and I – we did it on our own. It was like I told Pamela Stephenson, we were just kids ourselves. Neither of us knew what made a 'normal' family. We were just two crazy kids, learning together. Ozzy's parents were dead, and so were mine. I couldn't pick up the phone and call my mum and ask her for advice if one of my babies was sick. I had to work it out for myself.

It could be very lonely. It's so hard bringing up kids

without your family to support you. But Ozzy and I managed, and we raised three beautiful kids, and they filled my world.

So when my father came back into my life, it was very strange. Because I'd already done my grieving and come out the other side. My life had moved on. There were other people who I cared about and who cared about me. I saw him, sure, and when he got really sick I made sure he was well looked after. I paid the bills. He had my financial support. But he didn't have me. It was too late.

Maybe that sounds hard, but as you grow old you realise how little time we have. And time spent with my father was time taken away from the people who truly mattered to me. Who loved me for who I was, and who supported me no matter what. That's what it's all about in the end – time. We're battling it from the moment we're born.

It was strange for another reason too. He was not the same man I remembered. My father had been such a powerhouse, he was so strong. He had a presence, this force that came from him. He could walk into a room and heads would turn. You would hear the whispers, 'Oh my God, that's Don Arden.' That was how I remembered him. But then this little old man came into the room, who knew something had happened to his brain, knew he had Alzheimer's, and he was trying desperately hard to keep some control over what was coming out of his mouth. And, of course, he couldn't. And when I looked in his eyes, he looked scared. Vulnerable. And that wasn't my father. My father's eyes had been just so powerful – you would look into them and you would be terrified. Seeing him again after all those years, it was so sad. He was a broken, lonely old man.

So when the call finally came – that my father didn't have long to live – I didn't know how to feel. Because my father – the father I knew – had died a long, long time ago.

The first Free Ozzfest began on 12 July 2007 in Auburn, Seattle. I stayed for the second date – also near Seattle – and watched my husband perform to an ecstatic crowd of adoring fans, then headed back to England once more. For the next eight days, as for the previous six weeks, I seemed to sleep only on planes. At least when you're up in the air there are no emails to deal with, no phone calls to make or answer. It's when you land that the problems begin.

I dropped briefly in at Welders before driving straight up to Sheffield where the next day we had *X-Factor* auditions. Meanwhile – halfway across the world – Ozzy got in his tour bus and Ozzfest moved to Sacramento in northern California.

From the moment I landed, my cell phone never stopped ringing. Calls from LA, calls from Ozzfest, calls from the family. Then there were the calls from Dari about my father. She was with 'Mr Don' pretty much all the time now, sleeping on a camp bed in his room at Belmont. He was in a very bad way, she said. He had stopped eating. He was being given water on a sponge. Our doctor went in daily, but all anyone could do now was keep him comfortable. It was just a matter of time. Every time the phone rang, I felt my muscles tense. But my father was stubborn till the last.

On the afternoon of 18 July we drove from Sheffield to Birmingham. Some publicity shots to remind the boys and girls that *The X-Factor* was coming to town, and then we wrapped, ready to start all over again in the morning with the Birmingham hopefuls. And still my phone never stopped ringing.

The Birmingham auditions over, I returned to Welders, dumped clothes, repacked and caught the next day's flight to Los Angeles. I spoke to Dari just before we boarded. My father was no better. I called the doctor. His death was imminent, he said.

The plane was two hours late getting into Los Angeles. Melinda was there to meet me and we set off immediately for Belmont. At one point they had thought they wouldn't be able to take care of him as his condition worsened. But, thank God, finally he was able to stay. By this point any change would have been terrifying for him – just awful. So – that was a small mercy at the end.

I phoned Ozzy as soon as I got in the car. He was at home, at Doheny. He was worried for me. Tried to persuade me to leave seeing my father till the morning: I was too tired and in no fit state to deal with the emotions it would inevitably throw up. But I knew I had to go and be with him.

At that time of night it took a little over thirty minutes to get to Hollywood Boulevard. Melinda parked in the basement garage and we took the lift. My father appeared to be asleep – if you can call it that – lying on his back with his head to one side. Dari was in a terrible state, deep shadows round her red, bloodshot eyes and so pale. Her own mother had died just a few weeks ago, and now 'Mr Don'.

I walked to the side of the bed. He didn't seem to be breathing. Gently I pulled back the sheet and looked at him. He seemed shrunken, so skinny that his rib cage was protruding from his body, and beneath it nothing seemed to be moving, yet he was breathing – if only very shallowly. Every so often there would be a noise, like when the bath is emptying and there is a gurgling at the end. This was the fluid that had accumulated in his lungs. What no one had told me was that my father had slipped into a coma. He hadn't moved, hadn't attempted to speak, had been unable to take water since the previous Monday, four days earlier. One eye was completely closed, and the other was half closed, but I could see the eye, I could see the colour of his eye. I could see his pupil.

The time I arrived coincided with the end of the shift, and the day nurses wouldn't be coming back till Monday. Two who had formed relationships with my dad over the three years he had been there were really sad; while I was there, they came in and kissed him and told him goodnight. And I thanked them for taking care of him, and being so kind to him. They knew, I knew, that he wouldn't be there on Monday when they got back. Nothing needed to be said, you just knew.

His body was very clammy, and together we pulled his duvet off and left him with just the top sheet covering him. We all talked in whispers around him, but it would have made no difference. Whatever you did – touching him, talking – nothing was going to wake him from his sleep.

Even when the nurses raised their voices, saying, 'Don, Don – we're going off for the weekend,' and they patted his legs and rubbed his arms, there was no response. No change in the breathing. Nothing.

It was only when the nurses were talking quietly to Dari and Melinda that I noticed a prayer book on his bedside table. I opened it up and there was his name written inside: Harry Levy, and the date of his bar mitzvah. That did it for me. All the pain poured out of me and I wept and wept. I had never seen it before. I never even knew he had it.

I started to look in his chest of drawers and I found his prayer shawls, each the same pale blue and white with fringes, but one much smaller that he'd had since he was a child. I took the child-sized one and, leaning over him, put both my arms round that desperately thin body, and as I lifted him the expression on his face changed to one of pain, and a sigh escaped from him. It was the first time I had seen any sign of life at all in over a year. But his eyes never opened. I put the shawl to his lips – because you're meant to kiss it before you put it on – then got his black velvet yarmulke and settled it on his poor old head. Lastly I put his prayer book in his hands.

By now we were alone. The nurses had said their goodbyes and Melinda and Dari had left the room with them. I sat on the bed holding his hands, the hands that I remembered, big and strong but clenched. I wanted them to relax and I said, 'Let go – just let go.' Other than his hands, everything seemed so small. His wrists were so thin I could nearly get my thumb and finger round them. I kept repeating, 'It's OK. You can just let go. Just let go.'

I had wanted to dim the lights to make it cosy, but Dari told me that the rabbi had said to keep them on, that the room had to be light when you're facing death.

Looking at my father with his yarmulke and his prayer shawl draped across him, his prayer book in his hand, I honestly thought, no matter how much he must have loved my mother, he has to go and meet his God by the laws of the religion that he loves, because that's what he believed in. No way could he be buried in a Christian graveyard.

We must have been alone half an hour before I heard Dari come in behind me, holding a phone.

'Mrs Somers,' she said. 'She would like to speak to you.'

Don's sister, my auntie Eileen. I hadn't spoken to her since she'd visited Don in 2003, shortly after I'd moved him to Los Angeles, and that had been the first time we'd met for thirty years, but I knew she'd been in regular touch with Dari and Meredith, which was how she knew I'd be there.

She asked how her brother was.

'Not good at all,' I told her. 'They say it's just a matter of hours.' She asked me where I was planning to bury him. I explained the situation – that my mother was buried in a churchyard in Surrey, in a double plot. My aunt then said that Don had always made it clear to her that he wanted to return to Manchester to be buried, that he had even tried to get my mother's body moved to the Jewish cemetery there, but because she had never converted to Judaism, it couldn't be done, it hadn't been allowed.

'So tell me, Sharon. Where do you think your dad would want to be buried?'

'Personally, I would have thought Manchester.'

I sat on the bed, stroking my father's hand. Every so often I would hear the gurgling, the only sign that he was still alive. Around one-thirty I went home. Ozzy hadn't even seen me and Melinda was right, I needed some proper sleep. I kissed my dad goodnight and told him I'd be back the next morning.

When I got back it was gone two, but my husband was still waiting up for me.

Saturday was a big day for Ozzy – it was originally the reason I had planned to come back to LA the night before. The Ozzfest at San Bernardino is the biggest and most important of the whole tour. So when Ozzy said he would come with me to see my father the next morning, I said no. I wanted him to concentrate on the show, not to have to think about anything else. Also it was my emotion and I knew I had to go through it on my own, and the truth was I didn't want anyone with me.

The car engine was already running when the call came from Dari.

'I'm sorry, Sharon, she said. 'But your dad has just passed away.' She told me that she had been with him. That he never woke. His breathing had just stopped.

You read these stories about how a loved one dies, and another loved one will say I felt a shiver or I went cold at the moment they were pronounced dead. As if there was something that connected you. There was a time when my father and I were so close it was almost like it was tele-pathic. There was definitely a connection. And I always thought that I would know, I would sense it when he died. But I felt nothing. I was distressed when I woke up and generally very emotional, but when Dari told me I felt only relief. For him.

Eileen had already called twice, but we hadn't spoken. I'd sent a message via Melinda that I'd call her when I got to my dad's so I could tell her how he was. Now I had to call her to tell her that his journey was over, and I asked Ozzy to call my brother David. I hadn't spoken to my brother since Christmas

2006 and couldn't face the awkwardness. Later I knew I would have to, but not now.

When I told Eileen that Don had finally passed, the question of where he would be buried was top of her agenda.

'Shah, you are having him sent to Manchester, aren't you? Because he should be buried in twenty-four hours. If it's longer than that I'll have to get dispensation from the rabbi.' Jewish law is pragmatic. If it's beyond your control, then you do your best in the circumstances.

I explained that David felt that Don should be buried next to his wife, and that I would have to get back to her.

I also wanted her advice. I knew that in the Jewish religion when somebody dies you wear black but you also tear or rip a piece of your clothing out of respect. I had already ordered a black suit and a white silk shirt and a black tie for my dad from Ralph Lauren and I wanted to know if I needed to tear some part of that.

She told me that the dead person is returned to the earth as they arrived: wearing nothing except – for a man – the prayer shawl and the yarmulke. She also said he couldn't be embalmed. Suddenly I was overwhelmed with the practicalities. A doctor was needed to provide a death certificate. Belmont wanted his body removed to a mortuary as soon as possible. I called Dari to see if she could get things under way at the Belmont end.

I still didn't know what to do about the burial. I wished desperately that it was not down to me. Yet again I felt alone.

Ozzy was wonderful – so gentle and kind and watchful. But the decision would eventually come down to me.

I called my niece Gina. I needed to talk to someone who really understood.

'I'm sure Don did love my mother in his way. But for the last twenty-five years it wasn't the love of a man and wife. It was the love of a friend, the mother of his children. He was living with somebody else for years and years. So how can it be right to bury them together?'

Gina then told me she'd spoken to her brother Nicholas, and that he had relayed a story of him and Don meeting. This was after my mother had died. Don had said, 'Please, make sure that they bury me in Manchester.' Suddenly I felt a huge relief. Everyone else involved could be said to have their own agenda. But Nicholas had no reason to take a particular side.

I knew I couldn't win. Whatever decision I made, somebody was going to be pissed off. But my instinct was that he belonged in Manchester.

Silvana booked the flights. I wanted to travel with Don's body. The earliest the mortuary could have him ready was Monday afternoon.

In the meantime I had the first semi-final of *America's Got Talent* the next day.

I sleepwalked through that evening's Ozzfest. Sitting in the tented area outside Ozzy's dressing room where I have been so often, security kept people away. They let a few through: Zakk Wylde had just heard. A couple of others. Word got round, as it does. After all, this was Don's world. As I said to Michael when we were thinking about what to say to the press: 'Don Arden was a pioneer, a maverick and a legend, and music was his life.'

Somehow I got through. Watched Ozzy do his set, then we drove back through the night to Beverly Hills, curled up in our wonderful double bed at the back. I slept all the way.

The people from the Westwood mortuary arrived the next morning. We were in good hands. But there were problems. BA said I couldn't put Don on the plane unless he was embalmed. He also needed to be in an air-sealed metal coffin.

I called Eileen to ask her to organise the dispensation. She would take care of it, she said. She still works for the same synagogue where Don learned to sing – she's been there most of her working life. She would also take care of security, she said, and wanted full details of when I would be flying in.

'Security?' I said. 'For what?'

'Because the press will be coming to take pictures of you.'

And then it registered. But this is not about me! It's about my dad. He was a man in his own right. He had a history, was very much his own person, and for good or bad he left a huge legacy. I put the phone down feeling as if I was going to break into pieces.

Just at that moment my friend Gloria arrived – or stormed

in would be a better description. I was just standing in the kitchen, staring out of the window.

'Listen to me, Sharon, you are not going. This is completely ridiculous. At this rate you're going to have a breakdown. Your body just can't stand this travelling, not to mention everything else. You're out of your fucking mind!'

'I have to go, Gloria. He was my father.'

'A pity he didn't treat you like a daughter when he had the chance. Remember, I knew him. So don't give me any of that. Is this yours?' she added, pointing to my holdall.

'Yes, why?'

'Just something I need. Ah, good, here it is,' she said taking out my travel wallet.

'But that's my passport!'

'Why, so it is, but you aren't going to be needing it for the next few days.'

'Put it back, Gloria! Are you mad?'

'Never saner. But you are. Or will be if you go through with this. Ozzy, back me up here.'

'I think she's right, Sharon. What's the point of your killing yourself now? Just say goodbye and leave it at that. He's not going to know the difference. Let the rest of them fight over his body. You've done enough, you really have. You gotta slow down.'

We were standing in the ruins of the kitchen at Doheny. We had decided to move home a while ago, and now all this had coincided with packing up. Everywhere there were piles of boxes and emptiness. I looked at it all and thought: This is insane. Moving house is known as one of the most emotional things you can go through, and I'm moving out of two: Doheny and Malibu, and then this happens.

'Don't go, Sharon,' Ozzy said again. 'You don't need this, you really don't. I mean, just think about it. All that shit raked up again. Press swarming like bluebottles over the corpse.'

Suddenly I was flooded with relief. I realised how much I had been dreading the disapproval and the arguments, the tensions between different factions within the family. I knew some people would believe I had chosen Manchester over Surrey as a way to get back at my mother. It just wasn't true. I knew that my mother absolutely adored him, idolised him. But I also believed that they had to take different paths to meet their maker. I just couldn't imagine my dad's funeral in a church with a church service. When my mother and father met their maker, then they would be together again.

There were flowers in my dressing room when I reached the *America's Got Talent* studio: from Simon Cowell and the executive producers. Before we started filming, Piers Morgan came by to offer his condolences. He had read my book, he said, so realised that it had been a difficult relationship, but that even so it must be an emotional time for me. The last thing I wanted, he imagined, was to be watching a load of variety acts going through their paces.

So we sat in our places in the centre of the audience, the Hoff on my left and Piers on my right, as act after act did their thing, the audience clapping when instructed, standing up, sitting down when instructed. I stared straight ahead, seeing nothing beyond the two names – always in front of me, whatever the act – DAVID and SHARON spelled out in neon.

I said goodbye to my father shortly before they took his body to the airport. He was lying in the coffin I had chosen, that had to be metal because of travelling by air. It was like he was carved out of marble. They'd wrapped him in a white sheet with his prayer shawl round him. I had given them his prayer book to put in his hands. Eileen had said she wanted it, but as I sat there I thought: No. It should go to David.

I sat on the chair they'd put beside the catafalque. I didn't cry. I couldn't understand why. The night before when I had sat on his deathbed I couldn't stop crying. I couldn't catch my breath. When I went home, I was still crying. And yet now here I was, and he was lying there like a piece of cold marble in his coffin. And I didn't shed a tear.

For the last time I asked for my father's understanding.

'I hope I'm doing the right thing by sending you to Manchester. But I'm in the middle here and I don't know what else do.

'This family has fought my entire life and now we're still fighting over what to do with you. We wasted so much precious time just fighting, and for what?'

I kept thinking back to all those needless resentments and jealousies. All the lies.

I kept asking him: 'Tell me what to do. Just tell me what to do' – as if I was expecting a signal from beyond the other side. But there was nothing. No clock struck. Just silence.

I kissed his forehead and told him that, in spite of everything, I wouldn't have wanted any other dad. The gifts he gave me – the knowledge, the experiences, even the bad ones, I wouldn't change any of it.

I took the prayer book from the coffin so I could give it to David.

Then I kissed my father on his lips. I said goodbye and that was it.

I came out feeling peaceful. I didn't cry. I just felt sorrow, terrible sorrow.

I know I made the right decision not going to the funeral. I had already made my peace. I had said everything I wanted to say to him. I had told him I loved him, that I admired him. And I had thanked him. There was nothing more I needed to do.

I'd had the luxury of holding him before he died. I didn't need to stand in a graveyard and see the empty shell that was his body as it was placed in some hole in the ground. The funeral would be a chance for others to pay their last respects, but I had already done that. I didn't care what other people might think. I knew that some would judge me harshly, but I knew in my heart and in my mind that there was no need for me to go. There was nothing left to say or do.

Since writing the above, I thought I had said everything that needed to be said. Sadly, that was not the case.

On 1 September, I was feeling quietly happy. It was a beautiful Saturday afternoon in California. I was reading through the manuscript of the book one more time, glad that I'd decided to play down the row over my father's funeral. My father is dead and buried and I didn't want to rake things up. I'd had a couple of calls of the sort that leave you smiling. First, that everybody had enjoyed that night's *X-Factor* and that Jack's third series of *Adrenaline Junkie* was about to be shown on ITV2.

Then came a third call from England. It was Gary. He had some bad news, he said. In England it was ten–thirty at night and he'd just had a call from the *News of the World*. They were running a story by my brother. It would hit the newsstands at midnight UK time. 'It's ugly,' he warned me.

An hour and a half later I was able to read it on the *News of the World* website. Not only David's version of the issue about where Don was buried, but much, much more. It went on for page after page: a bitter attack against me, but not only me – my whole family, my friends and my business associates. I buried my head in my hands. I was devastated to read such a vile and deliberate attempt to destroy my credibility and my social standing, but the worst part was, it didn't really surprise me.

It's not the first time in the last few months that I have been faced with an impossible situation. Which way to go? Reluctantly I have decided that, in spite of my earlier decision – and the words I have written in this book are proof of that – I must speak out. Not just for me, but for my friends, Ozzy and my children. Nor is what follows written with hatred – as David's must have been – but with sorrow and a heavy heart.

Despite the fact that I have helped David out so many times, he must truly hate me to have said what he did. I think that there is something truly pathetic about a person who would rather rely on the assistance of someone he detests than to try to survive on his own. I know it wasn't easy for my brother. So much was expected from him being Don Arden's only son. Unfortunately for David he was always in his father's shadow. He served seven months in prison for blackmail and false imprisonment of the company accountant, who they thought had stolen some money. This was left out of the *News of the World* article, along with other unflattering and unsavoury facts about him, that would have shown what he was really like.

In 1982, after years of family in-fighting, Ozzy and I decided that now I was an Osbourne. I didn't want to live my life with the Arden stigma and everything I detested that went along with that name. I could no longer stand being subjected to the ugliness that surrounded the Arden name. The only way we could survive was to leave.

For fourteen years there was no communication between us at all. Then, in April 1996, my brother telephoned me. He told me that he and Don had got into an argument that had become violent and at some point he had beaten him around the head with a rolling pin, which had resulted in our seventy-year-old father being taken into hospital in England and David himself being arrested (although no charges were pressed by my father). He was calling me because now he needed me. David had no money and no home as after his arrest our parents had turned him, his wife and his daughter out on the street. He had apparently been living with them for the last four years. But now David was homeless and desperate enough to call me after so many years.

The music business had not been kind to David. All the various projects he had been involved in had failed. The latest one – an industry drinking and dining club called Gaslight just off Jermyn Street in London – was about to go belly-up if he didn't have an infusion of cash. After some discussion, Ozzy and I decided to bankroll his club. We poured an obscene amount of money in to keep it going, but after six months even David knew he had to throw in the towel. After that, Ozzy and I paid for David to lead his life: household bills, school fees, dental bills. David didn't come cheap. Ozzy and I certainly did not have to do this, so why did we?

Looking back, I realise it was for the wrong reasons. At first Ozzy and I felt sorry for him. Secondly, I felt guilty as I had made something of my life and he hadn't, and, lastly, I liked the idea of him needing me. We never had anything in common, and just because you're related doesn't mean you're bonded. I knew my brother had always resented me, but it felt good to help him and I liked that. What really brought us together at that time was the only thing we had in common – we both hated my father. And so the years rolled on and the relationship was set. David was the one with no money but a million hair-brained schemes. I was the one with the cheque-book.

In 2001 the family dynamic had changed. I was living in America and we were filming *The Osbournes*. Life was good. Back in England my brother and Don were talking again and I learned that my father was not well. He needed a pacemaker and his mind was beginning to fail.

The tragedy of 9/11 made everyone take stock and Ozzy and I discussed the situation for hours on a long road journey back from New York to California. It was Ozzy who persuaded me it was time to bury the hatchet. That I only had one father and whatever had happened in the past, he said, 'You're a long time dead'.

I took my father back into my life with open arms. Although at this time he still had some money and was self-sufficient, I felt he deserved better and I began to pay for him as well. A rental flat in Park Lane was only the start. Soon

Don began to pressure me to find David a job in the music industry.

I did what I could, and in January 2003 when I negotiated my talk show in America, I insisted that David be hired as a segment co-producer. I reduced my own income so that David could have a substantial salary – easily enough to care for his family – but the deal was that Don would come over to live with David in America and I supported them both to the best of my ability.

It was only when I read the *News of the World* that September afternoon, that I fully understood just how much David despised me. It all comes down to money. Don's world – the one he and I both grew up in – it's all about money. David knew as of last year that my cheque book was finally closed to him. He sold his soul to a newspaper all for money and notoriety.

As for the 'feud' over my dad's funeral, my father had been in my care for the last five years. I had been the one taking care of him, both emotionally and financially. David had not laid eyes on him for the last eighteen months of his life, as he could not enter the States following a drugs-related incident. David had said that our father had told him that he wanted to be buried next to my mother in Surrey and my auntie Eileen strongly advised that Don should be reunited with his parents in death. My nephew, my aunt and my father's girlfriend, Meredith, all said that he told them that he wanted to be buried in Manchester. I ask you, the reader, whose word should I have taken? In the end, I went with my heart and my gut that my father's wish was that his final resting place be in a Jewish cemetery in Manchester.

I find it so ironic that for so many years of my life I had tried to distance myself from all of the ugliness and baggage that went along with the Arden name, and here I am, a lifetime later, spewing out private family affairs that one would never want public. David and Don (from beyond), unwillingly though, have pulled me back into the life I had so hated. Am I any better than them? I'd like to think so. But David thinks he has now exposed me and I have to defend myself.

I made a mistake letting him back into my life. I should have trusted my instinct.

Please God, let this be the end of the horrendous Arden family feud.

# 11

## Hidden Hills

They say that spring is the time for new beginnings, but for me it was more like late summer. I had started to notice the difference a while back when the light began to come back into my life – but now there was an added warmth to that light. A weight lifted from my shoulders – the weight of duty. A responsibility I had never asked for, and never wanted. I felt lighter than I had for years. Free.

Kelly is busy rehearsing for her new role in *Chicago*. It will be her West End debut. The photos of her in her black corset, with her glossy black hair, caused a sensation in themselves. I'm so proud of her – she's been working so hard. I know she'll get a huge buzz out there on the stage, just like her old mum and dad. It's the best feeling in the world. Jack's just finished his third series of *Adrenaline Junkie*, and completed a documentary about the London to Mongolia rally.

He called me this afternoon – he'd just arrived back in London from Outer Mongolia. Yes, literally. After two months in the wilderness he was enjoying the trappings of civilisation again. Namely a fish-finger sandwich. I could tell he was exhausted, but he wanted to make sure I was OK. I tell him I'm fine and not to worry about me. I'm doing great.

And then there's Aimee, who doesn't want anything to do with the crazy world of celebrity – and who can blame her? My eldest daughter is very private and I totally respect that. But I hope she won't mind me telling you that she is also a beautiful, brilliant young woman, and that I'm so proud of her.

I'm proud of all my kids. It's like I said – Ozzy and I came from very different families, but both very dysfunctional. We had to work out for ourselves how to raise a family. We didn't get everything right – who does? But all things considered, I think we did OK. We're loyal, and we laugh together and we love one another. Not bad for a couple of crazy kids who didn't have a fucking clue when they started out together.

And now Ozzy and I are starting out on a new adventure.

I'd redecorated the house in Doheny, but that wasn't enough. With the children gone, it had turned into a ghost house and we knew it was time to move on.

The last few weeks in the house reminded me of the final

scene in *Citizen Kane*. No old sledge perhaps, but just about everything else: dustballs scuttering across the still shiny floors, trunks, packing cases, boxes, rolled-up carpets and furniture all over the place, everything left unpacked marked with Post-its: orange for 'SELL', green for 'KEEP', pink for 'TO SORT'. I would walk past them and wonder if I'd done the right thing. All our history was there: a wooden boat of Jack's, Ozzy's stage shoes, Kelly's clothes on racks. If only somebody else could make these decisions. The noises were all wrong, footsteps echoing around empty rooms, the screech of Sellotape ripping, no dull thud of Ozzy's music seeping through the walls. The house had been bought by Christina Aguilera and her husband. They're a young couple who want to be in the centre of things and Christina totally fell in love with Ozzy's studio.

It's been a good family home to us and it makes me happy to think there will soon be a little person running around it again. But it was time for us to go. Especially Ozzy. He hates the feeling of being fenced in and not being able to see out beyond the gate and the walls. It's easier for me – I can always get in the car and go out for a potter. But Ozzy doesn't drive and he feels this claustrophobia.

Anything that isn't going to the new house or into storage has been catalogued for a huge sale by Julien's, a specialist Hollywood auction house that deals in showbiz memora-bilia. The sale will be dedicated to the Osbournes' stuff: jewellery, china, silver, furniture and all the other shit I've collected over the years. It comes from our three homes: the house on Doheny Road in Beverly Hills, the beach house in Malibu, Welders in England. We're not selling Welders, but I wanted to clear out all that clutter. I'm keeping a few pieces for the new house, but nearly everything else is going – except the pictures. I'm done with gothic revival meets Cape Cod, and how many silver candle-snuffers or sofa tables do you need?

I'm sorry to be leaving Malibu, but we just don't use it, and it's turned into a very expensive party house for the kids. And now there's been a change in the law allowing people to sell alcohol on the beach. I'm sure it will all be a lot of fun but it's not the peaceful haven we need, when we're looking for a break from our busy lives. Time to move on.

Our new house is in a place called Hidden Hills, about forty minutes' drive north of Doheny Road, twenty minutes inland from Malibu, at the westernmost tip of the San Fernando Valley where it meets Ventura County, and I just cannot wait. We'll be moving in just a few days now.

I started looking about two years ago. I'd been to see properties in Beverly Hills, Brentwood, Pacific Palisades. I'd looked in Santa Monica and along the canyons that cut deep into the Hollywood Hills – always keeping within my comfort zone – but nothing was right. Too big, too small. Too expensive. Too much traffic. Not enough land. No view. This time I knew I had to have a view. It was Jack who convinced me to look further afield.

'You know what?' he said one Sunday when he came round for a proper English Sunday roast. 'This isn't the place to get older in. It's not for you in five, ten years. You don't want to be here. Really, you don't.' He was right. Ozzy and I don't need to be near the clubs or the cinemas or the It restaurants. I mean, how long can you do all that? I first came to Los Angeles in the early seventies to work. That was Hollywood in its rock-pop heyday: the Rainbow, the Whisky a Go Go, the Factory, the Comedy Store, the Dôme. Forty years down the line it's still a young person's place, and all that shit eventually wears thin.

The last thing Jack said, through his wound-down window as the security gate slid open to let him out, was: 'Move out, Mum. I mean it. Really. Move out.'

Next morning I was on the phone to Melinda with a bubbling sense of excitement. 'OK, M'linda. Let's do it. Let's start looking further afield.' By chance she had a friend who specialised in that area, and the moment I understood how Hidden Hills worked I knew it was exactly what we wanted. The great thing for us is that it's a fully gated community, which has the status of a city, although there are no shops, just houses – about five hundred of them – and horses.

Once inside Hidden Hills you would never imagine you were in LA. There are no sidewalks, no street lights. It's like finding yourself in a 1950s film. As the whole community is secure, there are no individual walls or fences – everything has that open Connecticut/Boston feel. You see kids playing outside, taking their dogs for walks, riding their bicycles, selling homemade lemonade and cookies on street corners. It's very family. Most of the houses are like mini ranches – nearly everyone has horses and there are horse trails criss-crossing the 8,000 acres, running between the properties. The community dates from 1950. In 1961 they turned themselves into a city in order to avoid being swallowed up by greater Los Angeles. There are no celebrities, except for Lisa Marie Presley, who has lived in Hidden Hills for ever. That's probably why I never even knew this place existed. I'd never had a reason to go there.

When it comes to driving in Los Angeles, I'm hardly the adventurous sort. I can keep a car for four years and end up with barely 2,000 miles on the clock. Even now, I never venture on my own beyond Malibu or Mulholland Drive, the road that runs along the ridge of the Hollywood Hills, which is like the frontier between two sides of Los Angeles. Only in the last few months have I begun to understand how to get in and out of the valley. It's a whole other world over there. After the twisting and turning of Coldwater Canyon – up then down – it just spills in every direction: Woodland Hills, Encino, Burbank, Sherman Oaks, Van Nuys.

We looked at three houses in Hidden Hills and then, Bingo. Our new home comes with about three acres of land, most of it just grass but with a lovely rose garden between the house and the view – a view that defies description, a panorama across sun-scorched hillsides and greener scrubland, like the garrigue of southern France, with the same kind of plants. Not a palm tree in sight. And it's all open. The three-bar white-painted fences are there to mark out who owns what rather than keeping anybody out or in.

There were the usual negative comments from friends, like how hot it gets in the valley in the summer, which is true. When it's thirty degrees in Beverly Hills it can be six degrees hotter in the valley, while it's barely twenty-five degrees in Malibu where the wind from the ocean keeps it cool. There's a huge snobbery in LA about people who live in the valley, and it's social death to have an 818 telephone number, but I couldn't care less. The new house is about as high as you can get – right on the western edge of the community. After us, it's just wilderness, wide-open expanses everywhere you look. From the other side you can see the valley spread out as if you were in a plane. And to get to the coast it's only twenty minutes' beautiful drive down Malibu canyon. What more could you want?

I'm having only one spare bedroom in the house, that's all. (There is a separate guesthouse above the garage, but I'll use that as offices.) We're past the time when we need to keep a room for each of the kids. An empty bedroom only makes you remember when it wasn't empty. They all have their own houses now. Kelly has her little gingerbread house in West Hollywood, which she's had for a couple of years. Jack has his own place on Laurel Canyon and he's very happy there. As for Aimee, she has just bought a little place of her own.

Our house, built by a casting director and her husband, is also new, though the style is more traditional. It was built about six years ago and they've done it beautifully – so there's practically nothing for me to do. A fresh coat of paint here and there, and that's it. From the low, colonial-style outside you walk into a circular hallway designed like an atrium, with a wall of windows stretching up higher than you can see, empty except for a sweeping staircase that curves up to the left across that wonderful view. I'm going to keep it all very spare. I want air. I want space and light. Above all, no clutter.

In the basement she had a screening room, which I will turn into Ozzy's studio. It has plenty of space. It even comes with a dog-proof compound right by the house so the dogs can run around free and happy. But what did it for me was that the moment I stood in the garden I had this flash, this little voice in my head: I could see my kids getting married here, standing beneath the weeping willow, by the rose garden, the hills stretching on and on behind them.

They'll need a little persuading. Aimee thinks the whole idea is ridiculous, says it's too far away from her and Kelly and Jack, who are all on the other side of the Hollywood Hills. Even Kelly thinks we won't settle. What they don't understand is that we're making a complete break. For Ozzy and me, it's like a watershed. For the first time we will have the freedom of living in a house on our own after years of having people tripping over us, intent on doing things for us. We want to do things for ourselves again. Both Ozzy and I have

been working now for over forty years and you never kno~~
what's going to happen to you next. At this point it's time to
scale down. And the dogs will finally have a bit of freedom. I'll
put up one of those electric wires that keeps them safe inside
the property. To see Minnie rolling on her back on the lush
green grass does my heart so much good. I can't wait to bring
the others. They will think they've died and gone to heaven.

In the meantime, I'm pleased to report that whatever the
Queens of the Stone Age and all those other fuckers said, Free
Ozzfest has worked. Nobody was hurt, it wasn't an audience
of killers or twelve-year-olds or child abusers. I think some
people thought every paedophile in the world would turn up.
They didn't. And Ozzy's fans got to go in free, and that was a
good enough reason on its own for doing it.

Nobody from the industry has said, You got it right. And
that really pisses me off. At least we tried to do something different. At least we didn't follow the bouncing ball. But
ultimately I don't care if the response from the industry is
negative. It's the response from the bands and the fans that
matters.

Just the other night I walked across the stadium, between
the seated area and the lawn, just as Lamb of God were fin-
ishing their set.

'So what do you think of this fucking festival being fucking
free?' cried their singer, Randy Blythe.

A roar went up to deafen you.

'Only Ozzy and Sharon Osbourne would come up with a fucking crazy idea like doing a festival for fucking free!'

Another deafening roar.

'So what's the name of this free fucking festival?'

Thirty-five thousand voices answered as one.

'OZZ-FEST! OZZ–FEST! OZZ-FEST! OZZ-FEST!'


Randy's right. Ozzy and I have come up with some fucking crazy ideas over the years. Maybe that's why we're still together. We might be crazy, but we're a crazy team. It seems to work.

This summer we celebrated our twenty-fifth wedding anniversary. For all our married life it was always me who planned things, who bought gifts. But when my husband got sober, I stopped having to make arrangements on my own. So when it came to our anniversary, we planned it together.

I organised Ozzy's gift, of course. A piece of jewellery I had specially made at Garrard's. I own a pair of platinum angel wings and Ozzy loves them, so I had them make up a bigger pair, three inches long but in gold – my husband only likes yellow gold – set with white diamonds. But I didn't arrange what we did – I don't think the wife should. So Ozzy set the wheels in motion. OK, I have to admit that Silvana did a lot of the legwork, but it's a start. It's all part of his sobriety and taking responsibility.

Last year we had a great time at Christmas choosing everything for the kids. The first time he has wanted to be involved in that. What he never realised before was that, if you haven't bought the gift, you don't get the pleasure of watching the wonder on their faces as they open it.

There's a little clothes shop for children where I was getting things for Gina's babies, and Ozzy was getting his grandkids gifts – Jessica's children – and he picked out these little wellies and raincoats and umbrellas to match and he absolutely adored it. And it was the same little shop I used to go to for our kids and which he's now going to for his grandkids. Oh, he knows what he missed, but it's not something we need to discuss. He's just lucky he's been given a second chance. Now all we talk about is Kelly and Aimee having children of their own. The pair of us are just desperate to have grandchildren. It's pathetic how desperate we are. We are like the criminally insane.

Until then we just have to make do with the baby deer at Welders. Even if we're not there we always get a call when a new one is born. They're my substitute grandchildren until the real ones come along. They were a Christmas present to Ozzy three years ago: thirteen does and two bucks that I got from a safari park in the West Midlands. They weren't in good shape when they arrived but now they're thriving and we're up to twenty-five. There would be more – six were born last year, and now this summer it's seven – but we have to give the boys away. Once they start fighting they cause terrible damage with their antlers.

Not all my Christmas presents are so successful. One year I got Ozzy a Vietnamese pot-bellied pig. So I carried it in, ribbon round its neck, said, 'Happy Christmas, my darling,' and handed it over. He took one look and promptly put it down. Mistake. Big, big mistake. Next minute there was this seething mass of dogs and in the middle this tiny little piglet. When I started to scream, Ozzy plunged in to pull it out and then held it upside down by the legs, which we all thought was cruel but he said was to calm it down. The kids were screaming, I was screaming and Ozzy was standing at the sink with the blood pouring out of this thing's head screaming, 'Somebody call the fucking vet!'

So the vet arrives and seeing Ozzy holding this pig upside down, thinks he's an expert. He used to work in an abattoir, which is how he knew what to do. It cost a fortune to have it sewn up, and then we gave it away. As Ozzy said, 'People think it's cool to have a pot-bellied pig, but pot-bellied-pig shit is the same as any other pig shit. It stinks.'

So, we'll stick to deer for now.

In the end Ozzy booked a castle for our anniversary on the west coast of Ireland that Louis had recommended. I had been in Glasgow for a day of *X-Factor* auditions, and Ozzy had a show in Dublin. I flew straight from Glasgow to the venue, but just missed the show. Then it was back to the airport with Ozzy and a quick twenty-minute hop to Shannon. Dromoland Castle was just eight miles from the airport, down winding country lanes. Totally dark. Not a light anywhere. It felt as if we were in another world. It was one o'clock by the time we got there.

Our suite was beautiful, ancient stone and wood, with a huge log fire burning in a fireplace the size of a wall. And God, did we need it – the weather had turned wet and cold. They had left out fabulous fruit and pastries and salads and cheese and crackers – and the four-poster bed was strewn with rose petals.

Ozzy had already given me his gift – a beautiful Cartier rose-gold watch. He gave it to me the moment it was delivered. My husband is one of those people who cannot wait for anything. I absolutely love it and already find myself wearing it all the time.

As for Ozzy's pair of angel wings, they were a complete surprise. The way the jewellers presented it didn't give any clues. The box was much bigger than even I expected – it must have been a good eighteen inches long – and Ozzy couldn't make it out. Later he said he thought it might be a miniature grandfather clock. I said nothing and just watched as he opened it. He was so happy – he couldn't believe it. All those years with crosses and now he has angel's wings – it's the first time the jewellers have ever made the perfect pair. Three inches long and he loves them, never takes them off.

In the kitchen at Welders there's a sign above the door. 'Angels can fly because they take themselves lightly.' And that's what we must do now.

It rained all day and we never left the room. The castle had given us our own chef to come in and cook and the food was fabulous. The weather meant no walks, so we just talked. About how quickly the time had gone, how we couldn't believe it was twenty-five years. About how the children were young adults and how that makes us old. About moving house and what it means to us. It's like a whole new chapter.

We'll be living alone for the first time in our lives together. We have always had somebody living with us. This will be the first time that we close the door and it's just us. I can't wait.

I'm not expecting perfection. If there's one thing this life has taught me, it's that you can't control everything. Things go wrong – that's life. The trick is to keep going. Survive. Pick yourself up and show the fuckers. And laugh about it when you can.

But first of all we've got our move to Hidden Hills to sort out. You know, that perfect haven, that oasis of calm? I got a phone call from Melinda yesterday. They found a tarantula in the garage. Big fat furry fucker. Oh, and by the way, half the pool wall has collapsed overnight – no idea why. I called up my soon-to-be neighbour, asked him if I should be worried. Were there a lot of tarantulas crawling around the place?

'Oh no,' he assured me. 'It's not the tarantulas you want to worry about. It's the rattlesnakes. They get everywhere. Hundreds of the things. And scorpions. You have to watch out for scorpions.'

I put down the phone and started to laugh. I couldn't wait to tell Ozzy. Tarantulas. Rattlesnakes. Scorpions. All we need now are a few bats and we'll be right at home.

# Epilogue

I guess it's obvious by now that I'm a very frank and opinionated person. And that has won me both friends and enemies. When I was writing this book, it struck me that it might be fun to contact a few people from both sides of the fence and ask them to be just as frank and opinionated as I can be. We got lots of responses – some good, some bad. And they're all printed here.

'Sharon has been my friend for over thirty years. She's funny, clever, lethal and loyal, and I absolutely adore her.'

*Elton*

'For some strange reason I really like Sharon Osbourne – she is completely unpredictable, a little bit mad, but that's what makes her special.'

*Simon Cowell*

'She's tough, but fair. If she lived in the jungle, she would be the lioness, looking out for her family; if you cross that line, you're dead. She's straight talking, fearless, hard working . . . a great role model for women and plastic surgery. She always knows how to make an entrance. She's a good friend, very loyal.'

*Louis Walsh*

'Sharon is like her dog, Minnie: small, smart, entertaining, unpredictable and occasionally absolutely ferocious.'

*Piers Morgan*

'As a firm believer that Women . . . yes, Women . . . should be the Rulers of the World (not, I stress, RULE the world . . . there *is* a difference, you know), Sharon is the quintessential example that women can take care of business and look good doing it. Sharon doesn't need anyone else to define who she is. And she wouldn't stand for it, in any case. She may not play guitar, but Sharon is a Rock Star nonetheless.'

*Gene Simmons*

'She's bold, funny, fearless and affectionate. She's a joy to work with and a delight to interview. She is God's gift to the talk-show host, because in addition to all the stated attributes (and most important of all) she has a natural and spontaneous sense of humour. That said, I'd hate to be in her bad books. She is a ruthless enemy.'

*Michael Parkinson*


'She reinvented Ozzy with OzzFest, she reinvented MTV with *The Osbourne's*; there's no telling what she will reinvent next . . . Now, if she can only reinvent the music business . . . Sharon, we love you and Ozzy, and you are "THE SURVIVOR".'

*Tommy Mottola*
*Former head of Sony and co-owner of*
*Casablanca Records*


'I interviewed Sharon and fell in love with her, simple as that.'

*Barbara Walters*
*TV anchor and journalist*


'Sharon Osbourne is a complex character who has experienced many of life's difficulties. Although I found her treatment towards me on *The X-Factor* unfair, untrue and, most of all, deeply upsetting to me and my loved ones, I still like to believe that Sharon is fundamentally a good person. She's just a product of her circumstances. It has taken me a while to come to terms with all the negativity that I've been subjected to over the last few years, but I have a close family that have been a tower of strength. Winning *The X-Factor* was meant to be a good memory, not only for me but my parents. It still upsets me that they don't want to watch the video of that night because of what Sharon did. I don't think she'll ever realise how much hurt she brought to them. I have now married 'the reliable Volvo', who Sharon mentioned in the final, and we are planning a family. I guess I'm finally moving on from *The X-Factor*, Sharon, Simon and Louis. I never thought I could say it but I wish her sincere best wishes for the future.'

*Steve Brookstein*
*Winner of* The X-Factor, *series one*


'Sharon helped me love my "toxic titties", and helped me laugh and live in the face of cancer . . . you rock DIVA!!!!'

*Anastacia*


'Sharon doesn't like Endeavour any more. The feeling is mutual.'

*Ari Greenberg*
*Former film/TV agent for the Osbournes*


'She is a brilliant and unusual woman and very funny. She also knows her mind and is unafraid of what people think. Her taste is very fine and developed; she likes the quirky as well as the classic, but either – she wears it well. She is a survivor and a lesson to us all! Top Lady.'

*Theo Fennell*
*Jewellery designer*


'If you find yourself in a heated negotiation with her and you think you should have no problem having your way with this sweet-sounding little woman with the cutesy English accent, remember one thing as they rush you to the hospital for emergency reconstructive surgery on your sphincter – her real name is Sharon Arden.'

*Dave Kirby*
*American rock agent*


'She's sharp, shrewd, deadly funny and deadly loyal. What a rare, special bird Sharon is.'

*Jann Wenner*
*Co-founder and publisher of* Rolling Stone


'In the last decade, I don't think I've been asked anything more than, "Were you and Ozzy Osbourne really next-door neighbours?" And my answer is always, "We sure were, for three years – and I really came to like Ozzy and Sharon." My wife Shirley and I see, in their transparent love for each other and their kids, the same bonds that have kept us married for fifty-three years now! Sharon is Mama Bear; she loves and nourishes her brood – and you'd better not mess with any of them!'

*Pat Boone*


'She rocks my core
sister friend
super mom
British babe
I adore.'

*Rosie O'Donnell*


'Sharon is a woman who stands out in a crowd; she stands with her head high, with great integrity and honourability and, most of all, loyalty to all around her. Having read her autobiography and now knowing her, she shines even more in my eyes. To have survived her colourful life and still have an inner peace – I only wish she could now bottle it . . . I certainly would buy gallons of it . . . she is definitely blessed. XX.'

*Kelly Hoppen*


'Meeting Sharon, she is everything you'd want a woman to be – smart, kind, warm, funny – and a heart of gold. And, by the way – she's not crazy!'

*Jerry Springer*

'I remember back before anyone outside of Los Angeles knew who SYSTEM OF A DOWN was, and I had our StreetWise street teams FLOOD the Ozzfest website, requesting SYSTEM to appear on Ozz 98. We took an unorthodox approach, and it worked. Sharon replied: "What the FUCK is going on with this band and these emails . . ." in perfect Sharon fashion, and subsequently we got the tour! It is that very spirit that puts Sharon Osbourne in a league of her own. Her approach and perspectives are unconventional, and that's what makes her so highly effective. I have a personal love for Sharon because we both have a fiery way about us, and anyone who knows Sharon, knows they better be on their toes and ready for a scrap at any moment. The beauty is that her fight, her vision and zeal all come from a place of passion and care. When you look at what she's done in this business – whether it be the career of Ozzy, the Ozzfest Tour brand, her hit TV show, etc, one can only give her due credit for touching so many people and artists. She deserves tremendous credit for helping to springboard many of today's most influential rock bands including: System of a Down, Tool, Linkin Park, Slipknot, Pantera, Manson etc. Bottom line: Sharon Osbourne is a WINNER, period. We have all been blessed with a true Maverick in her.'

*David Benveniste*
*Manager of System of a Down*

'I dearly love Sharon, and she has been a great friend for many years.'

*Mrs Rhoads*
*Mother of Randy Rhoads*


'Sharon is brilliant, witty and wicked. She is a steel fist in a velvet glove and I have had the privilege to be caressed; and the misfortune to be hit.'

*Rob Light*
*Managing Director, Creative Artists Agency, LLC*


'The ultimate measure of a woman is not where she sits in moments of comfort, but where she stands at times of challenge and controversy. I can say Sharon has succeeded in all three. Don't ever retire – the world would miss you. Love you.'

*Doc McGhee*


'Sharon Osbourne is an inspirational woman. She holds the best of two worlds in her hands. In one, the spontaneity and fun of youth (anything is possible) and in the other, the wisdom and compassion she has gained through her survival instinct. What a woman! We all love her.'

*Jo Malone*